PERSONAL POWER PLUS FUSION

HOW TO WIN ARGUMENTS AND P**S PEOPLE OFF
+ SELF CONFIDENCE EVOLUTION FOR SINGLE
MEN

THE #1 SOURCE FOR INFLUENCE, SUCCESS,
CRITICAL THINKING, MINDSET AND SELF-ESTEEM

JORDAN ELLIOTT

CONTENTS

HOW TO WIN ARGUMENTS AND P**S PEOPLE OFF

HOW TO WIN ARGUMENTS AND P**S PEOPLE OFF

YOU DON'T HAVE TO BE SMARTER TO BE RIGHT. USE CREATIVE, CRITICAL THINKING. REFRAME WITH LOGIC AND HUMOR

INTRODUCTION

Hello there, how are you doing? Y'all good? I hope so, and I hope you're even better by the end of this book! That's the aim; the intent; the purpose for my writing it. But enough about me, tell me about you. What are your aims or intent? What is your purpose for reading this book? A little hard to give me an answer through the page, I know. So, just think it over for me, and as you read the chapters to follow, keep it in mind.

In the following pages, we're going to cover a number of tools and techniques from the world of neuro-linguistic programming (NLP) that will not only help you in the art of conversation and persuasion, but in every aspect of your life. By the end, you'll know everything you need to start winning every argument and knowing how to piss people off the right way. Let's face it, you're not going to get very far in life without pissing off at least a few people along the way. This is even more true when it comes to trying to change people's beliefs or alter their way of thinking to better reflect your argument points or point of view. Since this is one of the central aims of this book, and it's an inevitability attached to it, we may as well learn how to piss people off with panache.

Get ready for a journey through the world of conversation, argumentation, reframing, and persuasion as we learn about neuro-linguistic programming (NLP) and how to use it to become the conversation king or persuasion queen of your wildest dreams. As we shall see, the ability to be a wizard with words, or to be the context-setter of every conversation, isn't something that you either have or you don't; it's something that you learn. That something is exactly what I'm here to teach you about today. So, thanks for coming! Turn the page and let's begin.

1

THE GRASS IS GREEN AND THE SKY IS BLUE, ISN'T IT?

Hard fact: You can't get anywhere substantial in life without pissing a few people off along the way, and if you thought you could, sorry not sorry. At least you've picked up this book so I can show you how to piss people off the right way. By the end, you'll be able to break down and take apart any person's argument; dividing, conquering, and destroying them so that you get what you want.

Seems a bit harsh, I know, but with practice and the techniques we'll cover in this book, it won't seem like you are attacking someone or forcing your views on others. Rather, people will start to think of you as some kind of magician; a wizard with words who can successfully challenge what seemed to everyone else as being a cold, hard fact. Before you countered and proved them wrong, that is.

Is the grass really green and the sky really blue? Believe it or not, one can very logically oppose even these proverbial "truths". Just make sure to do so in a way that pisses people off in the right way. It can be very off-putting for those that are the target of your argumentative prowess. As such, it's important to learn how to read the signs that you are irritating those that oppose you in the wrong way. In other words, we need to learn how to piss people in a way that makes them love us all the more for it.

In this chapter, we'll begin by chatting about how to piss people the right way, going over the basics of how to correctly express yourself and assert your authority before diving into the benefits of pissing people off. Let's begin our journey into the world of Neuro-Linguistic Programming (NLP) and learn how to use creative and critical thinking, logic, and humor to win any argument. Remember: You don't have to be smarter to be right.

THERE'S A RIGHT WAY TO PISS PEOPLE OFF

Have you ever found yourself so worried about saying something that could possibly piss someone off that you have kept your thoughts and feelings bottled up? Or, worse, have you given in to the ridiculous reasoning of another because you have been too afraid of rocking the boat? Well, that's all about to change. Believe it or not, people will respect you a whole lot more if you stand up for what you believe in and air your thoughts and opinions no matter who may try to disagree with you.

Rather than being a doormat walked over in every argument, this book will help you to set in place the solid foundations necessary to develop the fortitude of logic and reasoning that sees you outmaneuver even the most argumentative of your friends and family members. The hidden secret of those that get what they want out of a conversation is that it's less about not pissing people off and more about learning how to piss people off the right way.

If we want to leave a lasting impression on those around us or leave the world a better place than we found it, we need to speak our truth. We need to spread awareness of our passion or personal cause as far and wide as we can. If we're continuously worrying about pissing people off along the way, we won't get half as far as we could have. People tend to lash out when their world views are challenged in even the most miniscule way. This means that you could be saying something completely reasonable, but because the person you're speaking to doesn't agree with you, you piss them off. They get angry and let you know it. Other times, people are just itching for a fight and waiting for any opportunity to jump down someone, anyone's throat.

The bottom line is that their responses have nothing to do with you. It's on them. Everyone is dealing with their own demons in life, and it's not up to us to control the way they respond to what we say. Coming to terms with this is the first step to winning each and every argument you enter. It also forms the foundation of learning how to piss people off the right way.

It's All About Communication

While we don't have control over the way that others think, act, and respond to what we say, we do have control over our own thoughts, actions, and responses. We can control the way we present ourselves to the world. This will, in turn, control the way the world presents itself to us. Want to get whatever you want served to you on a golden platter? Act like you deserve nothing less. Want to win arguments and piss people off the right way? Then start acting like it!

There is a little more to it than that, as we'll get to in the chapters to follow. In this section, we'll set in place some solid foundations as we cover the communication skills necessary to begin presenting yourself in the right way. Remember that this doesn't mean hiding your true feelings from people or becoming an emotionless zombie. Emotions, like worry, frustration, or anger, can help to emphasize your point and inspire your audience to take action. Rather than donning a mask, embody your points, expressing yourself clearly, assertively, and with a pinch of panache. Let's go through the main tips and techniques you can use to up your communication game straight away!

Speak Clearly, Act Assertively

As we mentioned above, to begin pissing people off the right way, you first need to learn to communicate in a clear, assertive manner. This will make you seem like an expert or authority on any subject. Being assertive doesn't mean you have to be aggressive or combative, but rather that you speak in a straight-shooting, no-nonsense way wherein you say what you mean and expect to get what you want. Assertiveness allows you to speak about positive or negative topics without being hurtful or letting people treat you like a doormat.

To develop your assertive communication skills, begin by being an active listener. This means that you need to actively *listen* to those that you speak to, rather than just thinking of what you are going to say next. Believe it or not, thinking of what they're going to say next is what many people unskilled in the arts of communication do in a conversation. This pisses people off in the wrong way. It makes them feel like you don't care about what they have to say; like they're some kind of soundboard rather than a thinking, feeling human. Linked to active listening, developing an assertive communication style also requires a sense of personal responsibility within any conversation, respect toward your fellow people, and honesty. Finally, assertiveness also requires an understanding of compromise and how to play the fine line between being assertive and being rude or obstinate.

Get Rid of Assumptions

I'm sure that you've heard of the saying: 'To assume makes an ass out of you and me." If you haven't, well, now you know. Another quote about assumptions comes from the philosopher Eugene Lewis Fordsworthe, who said: "Assumption is the mother of all mistakes." According to Fordsworthe, assumptions are only useful when you don't have enough information about something. If this is the case, then you should always try and look at it in a 'glass-half-full' style of thinking, gathering more info as you go along and ridding yourself of the need to assume.

Don't Condescend or Be Overly Sarcastic

Besides assumptions, other communication ticks to cut out are condescension and careless sarcasm. Being condescending means that you feel superior to those around you, and you let them know it through your patronizing style of speaking and acting. There's nothing worse than someone who talks down to you as they try to tell you just how wrong you are. This is a surefire recipe for pissing people off in the wrong way during an argument.

Similar to condescension in its ability to royally piss people off is being careless or overly sarcastic. To rebut someone's point of view with a sneer and a sarcastic answer is more likely to get you punched in the face than to win you the argument. Remember that sarcasm goes far further than the words you say. It also includes how you say it (your tone of voice) and your body language as you listen and speak. It's important to become mindful of the way that you speak to others, and to rein in any bad communication habits that you may have developed. Condescension and sarcasm are two of these.

Remember: Not Every Conversation Needs Be a Fight to the Death

The final thing to iron out if you're to develop the communication skills necessary to win any argument and start pissing people off the right way is to stop viewing every discussion or argument as a last-man-standing style of battle. Steer clear from shooting someone down with any form of personal attack. There's a big difference between disagreeing with someone's ideas or opinions and verbally attacking their person. These personal attacks include name-calling, stereotyping, intimidating, and bullying, as well as other forms of verbal abuse.

Linked to personal attacks is viewing every argument as a 'with me or against me', 'win or lose' verbal battle to the death. If you take this standpoint, you are going to end up alienating yourself from anyone who slightly disagrees with you. This often ends with both sides walking away frustrated and even more cemented in their beliefs. In other words, viewing every conversation as a fight to the death ends with both sides coming out worse rather than better for it. This is not the way to win an argument and piss people off the right way. At times, we all just have to admit that we'll never see eye-to-eye with the person we are arguing against. Doing so doesn't mean that you 'lost' the argument, but rather that you can recognize a lost cause when you see one. It also means that you are okay with some form of compromise, which is a key part of developing a winning argument style. If you find yourself intimidating your audience into silence or bullying them to agree with you, then you are definitely pissing people off in the wrong way.

And there we have it! A few beginning tips on how to start developing the communication skills necessary to win any argument. As we have seen, a winning communication style isn't one where you are overly aggressive or insult your opponent at every opportunity. This will only make people feel the need to dig in their heels and retaliate or to walk away feeling angered, humiliated, and frustrated at your rudeness. Whatever the outcome, their negative feelings will be aimed at you and your behavior rather than the subject matter you were discussing. If this happens, you have lost the argument. This doesn't mean you should steer clear of making your audience angry at all costs, but rather that you should make sure that anger is directed at the problem or pain point and not at you. Indeed, as we shall see in the next section, there can be some major benefits to pissing people off in the right way.

The Benefits of Pissing People Off

> *"Pissing people off is both inevitable and neces-sary. This doesn't mean that the goal is pissing people off. Pissing people off doesn't mean you're doing the right things, but doing the right things will almost inevitably piss people off"*
>
> — COLIN POWELL

Colin Powell, the former US Secretary of State, said it right in the quote above. If you want to get anywhere, you need to accept the fact that you're going to piss some people off along the way. This in no way means that you should go out with the aim or intent of irritating or angering people. Rather, it means you should accept the fact that, as politely and eloquently as you may speak your truth, not everyone is going to be pleased to hear it.

To begin reaping the benefits of pissing people off, you need to know the difference between aiming to do so and understanding that doing so is an inevitability often outside of your ability to control. Let's take a case study from the world of leadership. Imagine that you are in a leadership position such as, say, being the Secretary of State. This means that you are responsible for carrying out the foreign policy for an entire country. You definitely don't want to go into any meeting with a foreign power intent on pissing them off, but you'd also be doing a massive disservice to your own country if you didn't still say your piece knowing that it may piss people off. In this situation, your job is to piss people off as diplomatically as possible. In other words, to piss people off the right way. Just as this idea works for the highest branches of government, so too does it work for every discussion or conversation you find yourself in.

The bottom line is that being a responsible member of society means that you're going to piss some individuals, or even groups of people, off at certain times. To be a pro conversationalist doesn't mean aiming to make everyone like you all the time. That makes you a pushover, not a wizard of logic and master of debates. As Colin Powell says in his speech on leadership and victory in business and life:

"Trying to get everyone to like you is a sign of mediocrity: You'll avoid the tough decisions, you'll avoid confronting the people who need to be confronted, and you'll avoid offering differential rewards based on differential performance because some people might get upset."

If you try to treat everyone the same without taking into account their "contributions", then all you'll end up doing is angering the people who you want on your side. According to Powell, these are often "the most creative and productive people in an organization." As with an organization, so with any conversation. Don't shy away from standing up for what you believe in because, chances are, there are many other people who think the same as you and will be in your corner if you prove yourself to be a skilled mouthpiece for their beliefs and opinions. What would you rather? To be criticized by people on your side and thought of indifferently by those you tried to appease, or to be criticized by the opposition but lorded by those in your corner. This is the 'benefit' of pissing people off, or, at least, why it shouldn't be avoided in conversations, discussions, and debates.

2

YOU DON'T HAVE TO BE A GENIUS

Becoming a communication king or a logic queen might seem like something reserved for the geniuses around us. For those who seem to be blessed with the gift of the gab or with an IQ that would make Einstein proud. However, I'm here to tell you that this isn't the case. Most of the time, it isn't the intelligence levels you bring to the table or the actual content of what you say that matters.

What's, oftentimes, more impactful is the context that you create for your argument and the ways in which you emphasize your points. While it's nearly impossible to increase your IQ to genius levels and is extremely difficult to learn every nuance or factoid on a particular topic, this isn't what creates a pro communicator. If you think about it, geniuses are not renowned for being the best of orators out there. This is because the genius often gets lost in the facts and figures, stumbling over their words as their brains race ahead trying to logically solve the puzzle of the conversation. The pro communicator knows that intelligence and content come in a distant second when compared to the circumstances of the conversation or argument. The pro communicator knows the real power comes from context and, as such, focuses on creating, reframing, and changing meanings to fit their argument and audience.

In this chapter, we're going to cover the importance of context in communication. We'll begin by chatting about semantics, the branch of linguistics and logic that deals with meaning and interpretation. After that, we'll go over some top communication tips and tricks that you can use to start setting the context of conversations and lead people to see things from your point of view. Using the techniques we'll cover in this chapter, you won't need to have Einstein levels of intelligence to seem like the smartest, most charismatic person in the room because, at the end of the day, 'genius' is a matter of semantics.

THE THEORY OF ARGUMENTATION

Have you heard of the term 'argumentation' before? To use the definition from Merriam-Webster, it's the "act or process of forming reasons and of drawing conclusions and applying them to a case in discussion." It deals with using semantics (how language contributes to meaning) and pragmatics (how context contributes to meaning) to create the most convincing line of argument possible. In other words, it's the way we form reasons for our beliefs, justify them, provide examples and explanations, and then draw our audience to a conclusion so powerful they can't help but be influenced by our argumentative prowess.

Argumentation vs Persuasion

Argumentation is a theory or school of thought studied by philosophers and practiced by lawyers. It's useful for anyone who deals with rhetoric (the art of persuasion), dialectic (the art of investigating opposing opinions), and logic (the art of assessing validity). We'll get more into these three disciplines in a little bit, but let's first begin with a quick chat about the difference between argumentation and persuasion.

As we just covered above, argumentation deals with persuasion through rhetoric, but that's not all that it's about. Similarly, it's tough to persuade anyone of anything without knowing a bit about how to argue your point properly, but the skill of persuasion is about more than just that. It's easiest to think about it in the form of writing. An argumentative essay, article, or speech is very different to a persuasive one. For one thing, a persuasive piece can be primarily emotive, using personal stories and powerful images to sway the audience through emotion. An argumentative piece, on the other hand, has to back up its claim with facts and figures, research and evidence. Emotion doesn't come into argumentation. Now, while we are separating persuasion and argumentation quite severely here, that's just to show you the difference between the two. To win every argument and piss people off in the right way, you'll need to use a mixture of many different methods, all of which we will cover in this book. Two of these are persuasion and argumentation.

The Goals of Argumentation

The theory of argumentation has many uses, reaching far beyond just being able to win any argument that you enter. It also teaches critical thinking and how to use correct logic, which will serve you in every aspect of your life. To develop your argumentative skills, all you have to do is practice the three elements, or goals, of argumentation. They are:

- **Identify the Situation**

The first step of argumentation theory is to identify the setting and situation surrounding the discussion or debate. This is where you 'read' your audience and decide on the best way to win them over to your side.

- **Analyze the Flow of the Discussion**

Once you've identified the argumentation situation and decided on the best way forward, the next thing to do is analyze your audience's responses and read the flow of the conversation. To become a fluent practitioner of argumentation theory, you not only need to develop your speaking skills, but also your listening skills. You also need to have a deep understanding of body language and how to read it, which we'll get to later on in this book. While you shouldn't change your beliefs or opinions to fit the audience (your aim is to change theirs, after all), you should change up your approach if you see the audience isn't connecting with your style of argumentation.

- **Evaluate the Arguments**

The final goal of argumentation theory is to do with evaluation. As a theory that draws substantially from the idea and ideals of logic, it's important to build critical reflection and evaluation into your use of it. This means both reflecting on your own arguments, as well as those of your opponents. It's also massively beneficial to reflect on the audience's response to the content and delivery style of your argument. Once that's done, determine if you managed to influence anyone's beliefs more towards yours. Then, make improvements to your argumentative approach accordingly.

THE IMPORTANCE OF CONTEXT IN COMMUNICATION

As I'm sure you already know, we humans are a social species. Our ability to communicate and collaborate with one another has been almost as important as our ingenuity in getting us hairless apes to the top of the food chain. In fact, many ingenious moments in human history were only able to happen because some genius was able to communicate their ideas with other people in a way that those other people could understand and act upon. But, as we said at the beginning of this chapter, you don't need to be a genius to win arguments, reframe situations, and get what you want out of a situation. If you think about it, though, most geniuses aren't really renowned for their conversation skills, are they? For some, the mere thought of public speaking gives them the cold sweats. This means that it's easier for us 'Average Joes' to master the art of conversation and communication than it is for the majority of geniuses out there. If you're one of those rarities who has both the gift of the gab and the gift of genius, please use your powers to make the world a better place!

Setting the Context

From the moment we wake up until the time we fall asleep, we are constantly communicating. It could be talking to friends and family, sending a message to someone on your phone, creating or commenting on social media posts, having a chat in the coffee shop with a complete stranger, presenting to a client, sending an email updating your team; the list of possible communications we could have in a single day is endless.

Even though we are always communicating, this doesn't mean that we always do it right. At times, the communication stream flows effortlessly from communicator to receiver, with the message or aim of the conversation being clear and easy to understand. Other times, though, there seems to be nothing we can do to make the receiver understand what we are trying to say, or we receive a message that makes absolutely no sense or seems completely illogical to us. What decides the difference between the two? The context of the communication.

Putting communication in the correct context is critical for making sure that the messages we put out into the world are understood and interpreted correctly. Context lets the listener know what the reason for or importance of your communication is, and provides them with the background information necessary to accept certain assumptions dealing with the conversation topic. The best thing that context does, though, is give your message meaning, deepening and broadening the receiver's understanding and allowing for a true conversation to develop.

Let's go over some top tips on how you can start setting the context like a pro communicator in every conversation or communication that you have!

- **It Starts With Perspective**

To begin setting the context, you first need to nail down what your audience or receiver's perspective looks like. Have you heard the quote, "Walk a mile in someone else's shoes," before? It comes from a poem called *Judge Softly,* written in 1895 by American author, preacher, and suffragist, Mary T. Lathrap. Lathrap ends her poem on the need to understand another's perspective rather than judge them with the line: "Take the time to walk a mile in his moccasins."

To step into the shoes of your audience, think about things from their point of view. Consider the way that they would interpret what you're trying to say. If you were them, what would you need to know in order to understand the context of the message you are conveying? What background information would help them to further understand what you're saying and, thereby, help to further your own agenda? Spend some time analyzing your audience and trying to figure out what their responses will be. This is how you can start setting the context and framing your argument with your audience in mind.

- **Balance the Power Dynamics**

Have you ever had a conversation with someone who continuously, if unknowingly, speaks over or down to people? It's the worst! And is dead certain to piss people off in the wrong way. By acting like you know more than the person you're speaking to, you put people on the defensive. This means they'll be less likely to open up, and highly unlikely to see things from your perspective, nevermind change theirs (which is our aim). It also creates an imbalance of the power dynamic in the people involved in the conversation, turning it into more of a battlefield where everyone is either vying for power, feeling threatened, or getting defensive. Rather than a battlefield, turn the conversation into a dance of which you are the maestro. Be open, see things from all points of view, and grade the complexity of your language and points according to the context and company in which you find yourself.

While Albert Einstein might have been a genius not renowned to be a spectacular orator, he does have a great quote that says: "If you can't explain it to a six-year-old, then you don't understand it yourself." By this, Einstein didn't mean that you should treat every person you talk to as if they are six years old, but rather that it's not about showing what you know about something. Rather, it's about ensuring the person, or people, you're talking to are able to understand what you're trying to say. This is how you become the balancer of the power dynamics, and the maestro of the dance that is a conversation.

- **Solve Their Pain Points**

There's a term in marketing and business known as the 'pain point'. This is the problem that the customer has that is solved by the product or service a business provides. If you are to master the art of setting the context in a conversation, you need to learn how to hone in on your audience's pain points. We covered a major pain point in the point above when we mentioned how it pisses people off in the wrong way when someone acts like they know more than the person they're talking to, and doesn't share that information. Feeling like they are left out of the loop or that they don't know some important piece of information is one pain point you can start solving for your 'customers' today. Providing an answer to your audience's pains, problems, and fears allows you to win them over through removing ambiguity and anxiety from their lives.

- **Be Proactive**

Linked to honing in on your audience's pain points is addressing them in a proactive manner. Doing so will help your audience to see the benefit of listening to you, help them to process what you've got to say faster, and make decisions or take action which is more in-line with your agenda than their initial one was. It's important to be proactive when communicating in context. The goal is to try to anticipate the questions your audience may think and to ask or answer them before they think to raise it in the conversation. Through doing so, you'll make people feel like you just 'get them', helping them to feel relaxed, comfortable, and ensuring that they're primed for reaching the conclusion you have planned for them.

And there you have it! A theory that will make you seem like a genius (argumentation), and proof that you don't need to be a genius to be a pro communicator. You just need to practice putting your audience first and know how to set the context of the communication. In the next chapter, we'll move on to how to enhance your creative and critical thinking skills through learning the difference between a map and a territory as we discover the power of mind mapping. Let's go!

3

MIND MAPPING

Mistaking the map for the territory. Believe it or not, this is what a lot of people do. Not literally, of course, but in terms of the way they see their own 'map' of reality rather than the thing itself. That 'map' is our internalized perception of the world around us, our beliefs, and our interpretation of reality. In a way, we all rely on our own maps to make sense of the world around us. In other words, there is no perfect, all-encompassing map or version of reality. A bit deep for Chapter 3, I know, but bear with me.

By its nature, a map is only a representation and will always fall short of being completely accurate or realistic. As with the map, so with our view of reality. The five senses through which we experience the world around us—sight, hearing, touch, smell, and taste—

sends sensory information through our nervous system to our brains, which then use that info to create a representation of the world around us, according to the data it has received, complete or not. What does this have to do with winning arguments and pissing people off in the right way, you may ask. Well, first of all, it allows you to step outside of the box of only having one map of reality. This allows you to control, and even choose, how you see the world, as well as to easily see and interpret things from someone else's point of view, which, as we saw in the previous chapter, is a key part of setting the context of the communication. Secondly, it frees you of the logical fallacy known as 'mistaking the map for the territory'.

In this chapter, we're going to go over the main ways you can start separating the territory that is reality from the mental map that is your sensory representation of it. We'll outline why it's considered a logical fallacy to mistake the map for the territory before moving on to how you can create your own mental map of reality using mind-mapping.

OF MENTAL MAPS AND REAL TERRITORIES

As we mentioned above, mistaking the map for the territory is a common logical fallacy that many people fall for, often without even knowing it. This kind of flawed logic or argumentative error usually takes place when a person confuses the semantics of a word (what it means) with the thing it represents (what it really is). By 'logical fallacy', we mean some error in logic that stops your argument from being logically sound. This doesn't mean the argument isn't persuasive and can't sway the minds and hearts of your audience. It does mean, though, that you are going to come up second-best to someone who is aware of the fallacy, and won't be able to poke holes in the arguments of those that fall prey to it, too. So, my pro orator in the making, that is why learning about such logical fallacies is important for those looking to win every argument and piss people off in the right way. Separating the 'map' from the 'territory' is also a freeing way to think of communication and life in general. Let's begin with the explanation.

Re-map to Increase Your Options

If you take to heart that every map is, by its very nature, only an inaccurate summary of the territory it represents, you have taken the first step towards increasing the options available to you in any conversation or communication. This is because it allows you to take a step back, separate yourself from your mental map of reality, and remap to the context you find yourself in and/or are trying to set. Remapping takes the idea of viewing things from a different perspective to the next level and is a great technique for winning arguments. Through viewing things from your audience's 'map', you'll also know how to piss them off in just the right way so that they love you all the more for it.

Remember that everyone creates their maps of reality through their five senses. In neuro-linguistic programming (NLP) terms, these are called our 'representational systems'. It's through our internal senses that we 're-present' (present again) the external world. While it's impossible for you to fully see the mental map of the person you're talking to (you can't know every experience that they've had, after all), you can build a map of them as the conversation develops.

Ways to Start Separating the Map From the Territory

Understanding the difference between the map and the territory gives you the freedom to draw your own maps and make them as large-scale or localized as you want or need in a certain context. It increases your options in any given situation to no end, with your imagination being the only limit. Let's go over a few top tips on how to analyze your audience and ensure you are tailoring the map of the conversation in a way that perfectly fits their own representation of reality.

It's All in the Eyes

Whoever said, "The eyes are the window to the soul," was on to something. I'd change it up a bit for this book, though, and say, "The eyes are the window to your audience's mental map." We talk a lot more with our bodies than many people give credit. These are the people uninitiated in the ways of neuro-linguistic programming though, and as such, aren't me, and soon, won't be you either.

In NLP, body language related to the eyes and eye patterns are called 'eye accessing cues'. Although there's still quite a bit of conjecture as to whether eye accessing cues are universal or not, there are some main ones that are thought to be 'common. These are:

- **Upwards for Visuals**

When people look upwards, they are visualizing something. If their eyes briefly move upwards during a conversation, they are letting you know they can imagine what you are saying and are keeping up with you and the conversation. When a person's eyes move up and to the left, it's a cue that they're remembering visuals, drawing on things they have seen and experienced. When a person's eyes move up and to the right, this is a cue that they are creating visuals rather than remembering them.

- **Level for Auditory**

When someone is staring straight-on, this is a sign they are processing auditory information. If you look straight and to the left, you are remembering sounds, while level and to the right means you are creating sounds. Constructed audio includes things like asking your audience to imagine the sound of pages turning or the wind rustling through leaves.

- **Down and Right for Kinesthetic**

If the person you're speaking to looks down and to the right, this is a sign that they're accessing their inner emotions or feelings. By extension, it could also mean that the person you're speaking to has understood what you're saying, is processing what you have said, or is connecting to your message.

- **Down and Left for Internal Dialogue**

The final common eye pattern is looking down and left, which is a sign that a person is speaking to themselves. Also known as 'internal dialogue', this often means that the person you're talking to isn't focusing or listening intently, because they are busy having a discussion with themselves.

As you can see, the eyes are indeed a window into the inner workings of a person's thoughts, feelings, and connections with your message or what you are speaking about. Now that you know about these common eye patterns, you don't only have to use them in observation, but can use them to bring on certain thought processes. Want to create an imaginary situation or hypothetical circumstance? Look top right. Want to remember some image or event from your past? Look top left. It's the same with auditory and kinesthetic processes, and even with bringing on a state of internal dialogue. With NLP, you can use it to not only read your audience better, but to also read yourself better and learn to set the context that brings on a certain state, internal or external. It's also one helluva great way to begin separating the map from the territory.

Learn to be an Active Listener

After the eyes, the next best way to tailor the map to fit your audience's representation of reality is to develop the skill of listening. Most of us think that we listen to someone else when they talk, but what we're really doing is thinking of what we're going to say next. It's a natural human thing to do because we place more importance on what we have to say compared to what someone is saying to us. It's our map through which we see, hear, feel, taste, and touch reality, after all, not someone else's. This is the viewpoint of someone who confuses the map for the territory and, as such, isn't for me and isn't for you. Rather than always thinking how you can fit what someone is saying into your representation, think about how what they're saying tells you more about their world view and how you can use this to better tailor what you're saying to get the result you're after.

The way to become an active listener is to practice being fully present in a conversation. Focus on what the other person has to say and actively *listen*. When we listen to what someone is saying during a conversation, there are always two goals. The first is to take in the overt meaning of what the person is saying and understand the emotion behind their words. The second is to show interest, engage with the meaning of their words, and display a general care for what the other person has to say. If you are just doing the first part, you're failing the task of actively listening, and the same with if you only do the second. It takes two to tango, just as it takes you being both a speaker and a listener in conversation as you dance out a dialogue with your conversation partner, or partners.

Linked to the two goals we mentioned above are the three aspects of active listening. They are:

- **Cognitive**

The cognitive aspect deals with the brain and the intake of information. This is the part that most people associate with listening but goes a bit deeper than the simple description given in the sentence before. When we pay attention to what people are saying, we take in both the explicit (external) and implicit (internal) meaning to their words, comprehend the message as a whole, and work this information into the context of the conversation and your surroundings.

- **Emotional**

After the cognitive comes the emotional. This doesn't mean breaking down, crying, ranting, or raving while the other person is telling you their tale. Quite the opposite, in fact. To be an effective active listener, we need to become aware of our emotional responses and learn to control them. Be cool, stay calm, and portray compassion rather than annoyance or boredom when someone is speaking to you.

- **Behavioral**

Linked to the emotional aspect of active listening is the behavior. Just as you should manage your emotional responses during a conversation, so should you manage your physical reactions while listening to someone. It goes beyond just controlling your reactions, though, to knowing how to convey interest both verbally and through body language, for example, but more on this later.

Being an active listener is an important part of determining the context in any situation, and vital in your attempts to separate the map from the territory. This is because it forces you to focus on the other person and their 'map' rather than your own, but you can just as easily use what we just covered to determine if your audience is actively listening to you while you speak, too. If not, maybe change up your approach until what you're saying hits them just right and they can't help but be enthralled.

Read the Language of the Body

As we mentioned above, body language is a massively important part of learning how to read and set the context of the conversation. Learning how to read body language is also an essential skill for anyone looking to piss people off in the right way. If you want to become a lean, mean, argument-winning machine, you'll need to develop a deep understanding of body language and how to read even a person's most subtle cues, such as their breathing patterns and the tenseness of their muscles. We're not going to go that deep over here, but rather provide you with a few useful pointers on how to start using body language to perfect the art of active listening.

- **Look Like a Listener**

This might be a no-brainer, but I'm going to say it anyway: To be an active listener, you need to look like you are actively listening. As good as you may be at listening to someone while doing other things, that is more passive listening than active listening and, besides, is sure to piss the person speaking off in the wrong way. Think of the phrase "pay attention". You are paying the person speaking to you with your attention. Make sure you get your money's worth! Avoid checking your phone while someone else is speaking and try not to even look at your watch. Once you start paying attention to it, you'll quickly realize just how distracted most people in the world are. You'll also realize how much more people open up and bond with you if you actively pay attention to what they've got to say.

To look like a listener, focus on the person speaking by literally turning your head and torso to directly face them. Next, make eye contact with them, but not so much that it gets uncomfortable. A general rule of thumb is that you should maintain eye contact for as long as it takes you to notice their eye color. After that, you could maintain eye contact until you notice the eye pattern or direction that their eyes are in. Finally, lean forward so that you show you are engaging with what they are saying and want to hear more.

- **Open Up**

If you want people to open up to you, make sure that your body language indicates that you are being open. Opening up your body language has a lot to do with your posture and the way that you hold yourself. The opposite of an open posture is a closed posture. This is when someone crosses their legs or folds their arms, turning their torso away from the conversation. Touching your face regularly or hiding your hands away are also two indicators of closed body language.

In order to have an open body posture, keep your legs uncrossed when sitting and slightly apart when standing, feet flat on the floor. Keep your arms relaxed and hanging at your side with your hands in sight. Also, use gestures where you show your palms facing up, as this is a sign that you are inviting the person to carry on the conversation. Finally, tilt your head toward the person slightly, signaling that you're interested in what the person is saying, curious about what they could say next, or are still actively listening to the story or idea they are telling you about.

- **Smile**

Some of the most powerful weapons in your body language repertoire are facial expressions. Out of these, the most potent one is the smile. There is nothing more disarming, comforting, or trust-inducing than a genuine smile. Not only do smiles make us seem more approachable and willing to cooperate, but they also make us as the smilers feel great. It's very hard not to smile at someone when they smile at you. Try it for yourself, if you don't believe me. Make sure that you don a genuine smile when you do this activity though!

An authentic smile begins at the corners of the eyes, crinkling up as the corners of your mouth slowly raise, drawing your mouth into a smile that enlightens your whole face and fades as slowly as it was raised. A genuine smile is a superpower when it comes to conversation skills and active listening. As we said, smiling makes the smiler feel great as it stimulates feelings of comfort and wellbeing. However, it's very hard to stop yourself from smiling when someone smiles at you. So, smile at the person speaking, they'll smile back, you'll both feel great, and connect over this feeling of wellbeing that is a smile.

- **Mirror to Increase Agreeability**

The final body basic body language technique that you can use to enhance your active listening is to mirror the body language of the person that is speaking. When we do this, our bodies are telling the other person that we like them, feel comfortable around them, and/or agree with what they're saying. Think of mirroring as listening and responding to the non-verbal part of the conversation as you get in-tune with what the other person's body is saying.

Most of us naturally mirror the facial expressions, postures, and even gestures of our friends and people we are comfortable around. All that we need to do is become conscious of this and use it sparingly and subtly during a conversation to show the other person that you are comfortable around them and that they, therefore, should feel comfortable around you, too.

Body language basics out of the way, we now come to the end of this section here. It's been a wild ride of learning to separate the map from the territory. After that, we went a few steps further as we learned to re-map and set the territory (i.e., the context) of any conversation. As we have seen, re-mapping has a lot to do with focusing on the mental maps of other people (their representation of reality and how they interact with it). Through learning to read, and give off, the subtle signs that sway those you converse with into feeling comfortable and open around you, we can prime our audience for changing the way they represent reality or, at the very least, know when we've pissed them off just enough to be loved for it.

A MAPPING OF MINDS

Now that we've separated the map from the territory, it's time to focus on how to map out your own path to successfully winning every argument you enter and being loved all the more for it. We use a tried and tested technique to do this, one that I'm sure you've come into contact with more than a few times in your life, if only at school. The technique I'm talking about is mind mapping. Yes, you heard me; that diagram with your idea in the central circle and lines connecting to it with the different details linked to your main idea. A good ol' brainstorm. That said, the science behind mind-mapping goes a whole lot deeper than you think.

A mind map can be thought of as a visual representation of how our brain and neocortex function. In simpler terms, this means that our brains start with a central idea or notion. This is then branched out into sub-ideas as it goes down the neocortex line. These then branch out again and again depending on the complexity and detail of the idea. Understanding this concept allows us to make changes and take control of the more specific details, contexts, and circumstances; to create our own 'mind-maps' in the conversations we enter, branching out our ideas as far as is needed to convince our readers that we know what we're talking about and they should believe us. Let's take a closer look into this powerful tool for taking control of not only the conversation but, more importantly, your own mind.

Why Is Mind Mapping So Powerful?

To put it simply, a mind map is one of the best organizational thinking tools around. It allows us to map out our thoughts and remember long and complex pieces of information. Believe me, if you want to start winning arguments, you need to know what you're talking about and have points to back up your claim. This just goes with the territory of argumentation and persuasion: You have to know what you're talking about. In the past, you could get far pretending to know what you're talking about, but in the modern day, someone can easily just pick up their phone during a conversation and fact-check your claim before believing you. There's nothing more harmful to winning an argument than being labeled a liar or, to use a popular term, "fake news". As such, it's important to have a lot of real examples and actual explanations ready to back up your claim. Luckily, there's no need to write a whole essay or even read a book on the matter (although it's always recommended to read up on your areas of interest). Just take out a piece of paper, draw a central circle, plonk your topic in the middle, and then do a bit of research, connecting some interesting tidbits of information to your central circle as you find it on the web. Read over it once or twice, and you'll have those examples and argument points memorized, primed, and ready to be used to sway your audience during a conversation.

Beyond just helping you to become the smartest person in the room, mind mapping also helps to invigorate critical and creative thinking, structure ideas, heighten memorization and concentration, and even aid with making decisions and planning your way to overcoming any difficulties that you may be facing. Overall, it's a good idea to add to your argumentor's toolbox. Let's go over why exactly it is that mind maps are so powerful.

- **They Create a Map of Your Thoughts**

The first reason why mind maps are so powerful is because they map out our thoughts using a similar structure to the way the original thought happened in the brain. Our brain is one massive connection of neurons, billions of them. All neurons (aka 'nerve cells') connect with one another, forming a neural network or neural web. There are central nuclei, the neuron, that has thousands of branches, known as 'dendrites', leading out from it, many even connecting to the dendrites of other neurons. In other words, our brains are nothing more than a massive mind map, and it's a powerful thing to bring to any brainstorming exercise.

- **Color Stimulates the Brain**

If you thought you were going to make your mind maps in black and white, I've got other news for you. Monochrome is very monotonous for the brain, while color and vibrancy stimulate it. We literally get energized by seeing bright colors. So, make your mind maps colorful and you'll further enhance the amount of information that you manage to retain and that you can recall at a moment's notice.

- ## A Collaboration of Different Thinking Methods

Another unique thing about mind maps is that they combine a lot of different types of thinking. As we mentioned above, it's best to make your mind maps colorful. Added to the drawing factor, this activates our artistic and creative thinking. As we covered earlier, it's a representation of the way that we have ideas and make connections, which makes it an organizational science. Through creating connections between different ideas, we also activate our logical and critical thinking skills. Combine that with both words and images, as well as emotions, through colors and drawings, and you've got one potent think-tank of a technique.

- ## They Help Us Generate Ideas and Notice Patterns

The final superpower of mind maps is in helping us to draw connections between different points and even notice patterns in a single idea or between multiple different points. This part of mind mapping comes more from when you read over and analyze the map again rather than when you create it for the first time. Because it's not meant to be a one-and-done kind of job. Mind maps are generative, which means that they help us to generate new ideas through analyzing what we already know, noticing gaps or patterns in our logic, thereby improving and deepening our understanding of the topic. For memorization, understanding, and thinking over information, a mind map has you covered.

Creating Mind Maps

Although making a mind map is pretty easy, there is a bit more to it than you may think, especially if you want to get the most out of it. The mind mapping process that we're going to go over below comes from the renowned neuroscientist and communication pathologist, Dr. Caroline Leaf, and is one that works no matter the depth or complexity of the idea that you want to map out. Let's get your mind-mapping game on point!

- **It's All About the Input**

Making a mind map is part of the planning or researching stage of development. As such, you need to know what you are researching, and research it. The mind map should be the summary of the info that you read, listen, or watch. A general rule of thumb is that you should select about 15-35% from what you research and use this as the input for your mind map. Focus on a specific part of the research material rather than the entire thing; you can always create another mind map to deal with the other factors of the reading.

- **Create the Mind Map**

With your input information selected and at the ready, now comes the time to design your mind map. Get your blank paper at the ready and draw your central circle, adding as much artistry as you are capable of to make it unique and easily memorable. For me, there ain't much art going on in my mind maps, but I try my best to add a scribble or sketch every now and then to make it personal and to aid my ability to recall the mind-mapped information (through remembering the specific type of mind map itself).

- **Reflect, Personalize, and Teach**

After you have created your mind map comes the time to read over the summarized information and reflect on it. This is also a great time to add more color and flare to your mind map. Trust me, the more visually appealing the map is, the easier it will be to recall it and re-present the information embedded in it.

Another great way to improve your ability to remember the mind-mapped information is to discuss it with, or teach it to, someone. This will help to take the info from being stored in your short-term memory and upgrade to your long-term memory stores. If you can't find an actual person willing to let you 'teach' them or don't have a discussion buddy, no problem! Just teach it to your pet, your child, or even your house plant. Another option is to look into the mirror and teach yourself, or to imagine a person and teach them. Whatever and whoever you choose matters far less than the action of teaching back the information. Through this process, you won't just store the information in your brain, but start to link it with other mind maps, integrate it with discussion or argument points, and apply it in helping you win every argument you enter.

Welcome, argument king or queen in the making, to the end of Chapter 3! So far, we've been setting the stage for how to win arguments and piss people off the right way. We've learned the basics of effective communication and the importance of reading and setting the context of the conversation. As we've seen, in order to read the context of the discussion, you first need to separate the map from the territory. Only through doing so will you be able to read the map of your audience and the context in which the argument or conversation is taking place. We then went over the basics of body language and how to read it as we learned about the importance of being an active listener.

It's not all about reading the room and listening to your audience, though; you also need to impress them with what you know. That's where research and mind mapping come into play. A mind map is the perfect planning tool for us to use in our pursuit of winning every argument. It's quick to make, easy to populate, and visually appealing for our brains. It also reflects the way thoughts and ideas are stored in the brain, which you can reverse-engineer during a debate or discussion to create a mental map of your argument points in the minds of your audience.

In the next chapter, we're going to deepen your connection to your audience and your ability to influence their thoughts as we talk about the importance of feelings and the value of emotionally intelligent arguing.

4

EMOTIONAL RESCUE

E motion plays a huge part in the way that we humans see, understand, and experience the world around us. While the pure follower of argumentation theory might want to leave emotion out of the picture completely, that's not the way to win every argument. As we said back in Chapter 2, the best way to win arguments and piss people off the right way is to use a combination of argumentation theory's flawless logic and persuasion's potent emotive responses.

Just as emotions are an unavoidable part of being human, so is having arguments, disagreeing with others, and debating contentious issues. Should we keep quiet and not voice our opinions because they are different or completely the opposite to someone else's in the conversation? Hell no! Should we shout everyone down with the words "You're wrong, I'm right!" and get into verbal fisticuffs at the slightest disagreement? Of course not! It takes a balanced and well-rounded individual to tread the line of the conversation, standing up for themselves while simultaneously winning over their audience, pissing them off because they can't help but change their beliefs based on their argumentative rationale and persuasive prowess. It takes a person knowing how to read a room, set the context, and connect with their audience on a behavioral, intellectual, and emotional level.

In the previous chapter, we covered the behavioral side, as we learned to separate the map from the territory and how to be an active listener, and the intellectual side as we covered mind mapping. In this chapter, we're going to go over the emotional side as we learn about emotional intelligent arguing and why emotions are more persuasive than logic. Let's go!

EMOTIONALLY INTELLIGENT ARGUING

Believe it or not, our inability to see eye to eye is built into our very physiology. A study carried out by the Institute of Cognitive Neuroscience at University College London found that there are marked anatomical differences between the brain of a liberal and the brain of a conservative. Crazy, right? This doesn't mean that it's impossible to change our way of thinking, but rather that some beliefs or opinions are so deeply ingrained in our psyches that we don't even realize they're there. If you run the same train of thought over and over again, you're going to leave a track of it in the neural pathways of your brain. The more you think about that idea (and the certain viewpoint you have of it), the more enhanced and deepened the connection between the neurons becomes. It's important to understand this in order to overcome it.

What do you do when you come up against someone whose opinions are so different to yours, but who is also so ingrained in their beliefs that they refuse, or even mock, seeing things from your perspective? This is where emotionally intelligent arguing comes into play. If you know how to manage and control your emotions, then you can remain in-control of yourself and continue to set the correct context for winning arguments and pissing people off the right way. When we allow our emotions to run rampant during an argument or disagreement, it tends to end in the conversation going nowhere very quickly. This won't win you the argument. All it leads to are both sides hunkering down and getting ready for battle, verbal or otherwise.

How to Become an Emotionally Intelligent Arguer

The emotionally intelligent arguer views things through the lenses of rationality and productivity. Someone using this technique is not only much more certain to win over their audience, but also to strengthen the relationships you have with people, even if they disagree with you. Over time, these people will come over to your side, because you are always in control during a discussion and, with your knowledge of body language and the added knowledge you spread (easily remembered courtesy of the mind maps), you will always seem like the smartest person in the room, without being arrogantly so. When you remain calm during a heated discussion, it immediately cools it off. It shows that you respect the person that you disagree with and are actively listening to them.

Let's go over the main ways you can keep an emotional level-head even in the most heated of arguments, and how you can add emotionally intelligent arguing to your repertoire of argumentative and persuasive skills. Remember that the goal isn't to be emotion-free, but to be in control of your emotions.

• The Power of Questions

As we covered when we talked about active listening, communication is always made up of at least two, the speaker and the listener, with the roles interchanging as the conversation flows on. While most people may only focus on what they want to say next in the discussion, this isn't for a toastmaster such as yourself. You understand that people want to be listened to; yearn to be heard. This is never more so than in a heated argument. Do either of these sound familiar? "Let me finish!" or, worse still, "You're not even listening to me!"

These are phrases said in the heat of battle, when tempers are flaring, and the conversation is slowly smoldering into a raging inferno. To combat this and save the conversation from burning out or ending up in a fist fight, make sure that the person you are talking to feels heard. Doing this is simple; just ask them a question about their viewpoint or to expand or elaborate on what they just said. This will not only catch them off guard but can also go a long way toward changing their way of thinking. A great question perfectly placed in a conversation can help someone reach the conclusion that their viewpoint is wrong without you ever having to tell them that. Don't focus on your feelings too much (you already know who you are and how you feel about things), but rather act like a journalist (the good kind) trying to understand the point of view of the person you're talking to.

- **Listen Rather Than Plan**

As we've mentioned before, most people don't actively listen to what the other person is saying. They're too busy planning their next killer comeback or a rebuttal sure to knock the socks off of their opponent, but when they force their chance to speak and announce their undeniable truth, it falls on deaf ears. Their opponent isn't listening either but is already lost in planning out what they're going to say next. Break the cycle through actively listening to your 'opponent' rather than planning out your next move. You've already mind-mapped your argument points out to be implemented at a moment's notice, so focus instead on the other person and how you can change their opinion to better match yours. As you actively listen to your opponent during an argument or conversation, you'll soon see them start doing the same and taking in what you've got to say. When this happens, your audience is receptive to what you've got to say, and you can lay out your mind-mapped argument points on ears that will actually hear and take in that information.

- **Explain Your Way of Thinking**

Just as important as thinking about things from the perspective of the people you're talking to is getting them to see things from your perspective. This is where you show off your communication skills, describing your thoughts, beliefs, and ideas in a vivid, but simple, way that is understood and enjoyed by all. To do this, you need to simply ask yourself: "How can I best help my audience to understand my perspective?" Write it in the middle of a page, circle that bad boy, and make a mind map out of it. You may want to make another mind map with the question: "What's my perspective?" as its focus. You can grow it out from there to zoom in on your perspective for each of your different argument topics. Combine that with the information you research and how best to help your listener see things from your perspective on this matter, and you're onto a winning formula for argumentative success.

Explaining your way of thinking also shows your audience that you respect them, and, in turn, they will feel more comfortable around you and respect you the more for it.

- **Play the Long Game**

Changing someone's opinion or way of thinking doesn't always happen during the course of a single conversation, especially if it gets a bit heated toward the end. Rather than pushing an argument to its boiling point, display your emotional intelligence and know when to call it a day on a certain topic. This doesn't mean that you've lost the argument, especially since you'll be ending it because the other side is losing their cool. In your calm, composed manner of a context-setter and pro communicator, say that you think it would be best to call the discussion for the day. Tell them you'll reflect on what they've said, as you hope they do with your talking points, and that the conversation can continue at a later date. Then, actually reflect on their points; map them out and see if there's any common ground or workable territory for you to politely exploit in your next encounter. When you are ready, contact the person and see if they're ready to have the next discussion. Even if they say "no", you'll have gone up tenfold in their books for following up, and they're sure to listen to you far more actively the next time you meet.

EMOTIONS TRUMP LOGIC

As much as we may wish it wasn't so, logic almost always comes second when emotion is involved. There's no point denying it, and once accepted, we can start using this to our advantage. Bring both the facts and the feelings to the table, and you're onto a power-house combo of persuasiveness. Another harsh reality is that humans are not nearly as rational as we like to believe. Take smoking, for example. We know it's bad for us, we understand the facts and see the logic of that, but still, we light another one up, nodding our heads and saying "Yeah, these things are terrible for you," before taking another sweet drag. Not a smoker? It's just one example of many but goes to a central point: Humans can understand every part of the logic of something, but that's not enough of a motivation to get someone to change their beliefs. You have to add that essential emotional angle to it.

Emotional Do's and Don'ts

A study carried out by neuroscientist Antoine Bechara at the University of Iowa showed that patients who couldn't feel emotions struggled to make decisions. These are people who've suffered orbitofrontal damage

(damage to the front part of their brain immediately above the eyes).

Bechara uses a theory called the 'Somatic Harper Hypothesis' to show the neurological link between the disconnection these patients have with emotions and feelings, and their dire impairment of sound judgment and their inability to make decisions. What does this mean for you and your aim to win every argument that you enter? Well, if the emotionless can't make decisions or life choices, then those that are full of emotion must be primed to make these types of decisions. First, we learn to control our own emotions, and then we learn how to use the emotions of others in order to further set the context of the conversation and further our chances of not only winning the argument but winning them over to our point of view.

Here are a few emotional do's and don'ts that you can use as guidelines when navigating your listeners through the new territory of the conversation, adding to their mental maps as you engage and enthrall their mind, body, and emotion.

- **Choose Your Emotion Wisely**

When using emotion to win an argument, don't focus on a wide array of emotions, but hone in on a few select ones or, even better, a single emotion. You could focus on anger and get them riled up about the injustice of the world and connected to your argument point, of course. You could use humor to include a wider audience in the discussion and get people engaged in the conversation. Or, you could focus on inspiring people to take action. Which one you choose comes from when you are actively listening and 'reading the room' of the people you're conversing with and beginning to read and set the context.

• Steer Clear of Fear

One emotion you don't want to use is fear. Shared worries, yes. Collective pain points, definitely, but never fear. Well, only in very specific circumstances that are so uncommon that it's better to just say never. Fear may get people to take action, but that action is often frantic, illogical, and comes from a place of self-protection rather than being won over by your argumentative prowess. If you use fear to win an argument, then it is fear itself that has won, not you. Your job as a pro communicator should be to allay the fears of your audience by showing them a way out, rather than how far down they are.

• Develop a Memorable Style of Speech

I don't know about you, but when I think of emotions, I think of drama, which leads me to acting. Maybe that's just my mental mind map of that information link, but it covers an important point. If we want people to remember us and what we have to say, we have to put on a show. It's not full acting, as you want to connect with your audience on a personal basis rather than putting on a facade. Think of it more like yourself, your own personality, but enhanced, enlarged, accentuated whenever you enter into a conversation or discussion.

Animate your discussion points with gestures, paint vivid pictures with your descriptions and metaphors, and speak like you are the host of a party. If you are to set the context of the conversation, then you are, in fact, hosting that conversation. And so, take that part of your persona labeled 'host' and upgrade its mental map by adding 'host of the conversation' to the list of times it activates. If you are entertaining both in terms of what you say and how you say it and animate it, then people are far more likely to listen to, and remember, your message. Everybody loves a good show, after all!

With that, another chapter comes to an end. In this one, we learned how to bring emotion to the table in our conversations, discussions, and arguments, discussing the ins and outs of emotionally intelligent arguing before diving into how you can use emotion to best effect in driving home your message. In the next chapter, we'll be taking our knowledge of emotions to the next level as we learn about the power it has to leave a lasting influence on your audience.

5

CONVINCER AND BELIEVER

Where do your beliefs come from? While it can be difficult to answer this question, especially with the more embedded, ingrained ones, the bottom-line is that our beliefs have to come from somewhere. They definitely don't appear out of thin air, and we don't carry them over from whatever space comes before birth. In fact, there is quite a specific process by which we gain our beliefs. In order for our minds to accept a belief, it needs to pass the gauntlet of fitting into the way we see and understand the world around us. As such, it needs to link with what we already believe in, meshing together with sensory information to create the overall map that is our representation of reality.

Even if we understand that the map is not the territory and focus instead on setting the context of the discussion, we still cannot escape our beliefs. And why should we? Winning an argument doesn't mean that you believe in nothing but defeating the logic of your opponent, but rather sharing your beliefs and opinions, backed up with facts, explanations, and examples in a passionate and emotionally intelligent way that convinces the listener to change what they believe in, even if ever so slightly.

Many people go through life lost within their own minds. They never learn to read their own mental maps, let alone write their own version of it. These individuals let their emotional states control them, sabotaging themselves through stubbornly holding on to their self-limiting or past beliefs. Developing the willpower to believe something new or different seems impossible to these people, and indeed it may be. When coming up against such people, it may be best at times to just label them as a 'hopeless case' and move your focus on to people that you can actually engage with. But, if you want to slug it out with such people, the only thing that's going to work is to persuade them through emotion.

No matter how hard-lined or flexible the beliefs of the person you're talking to are, emotion is your best bet for winning them over. In this chapter, we're going to learn about the power that emotion has in influencing your audience and how to use it to get them to not only remember your message, but to take action and change their own beliefs based on what you had to say.

THE THREE KEYS OF PERSUASION

An easy analogy is to think of emotion as a key that unlocks your audience and opens them up to considering new possibilities. The art of persuasion, also known as 'rhetoric', has been studied and written about since the days of the Ancient Greek philosophers over 2,000 years ago. One of the first people to write on this topic was Aristotle, in his philosophical piece, the *Rhetoric*. In this groundbreaking piece of work, Aristotle covers three key strategies for persuading someone. They are:

- **Ethos**

Meaning 'character', ethos covers everything to do with the person speaking and their credibility or authority as a speaker. This includes the facts that you bring to the table, as well as the way you present the information and yourself. Body language and active listening also fall under ethos.

- **Logos**

The Greek word for 'logic', this strategy deals with research, evidence, and argumentation. It's where you back up your claims with facts and figures and lay out your argument points in a way that shows you have analyzed all sides of the situation before reaching the deductions you are telling them about.

- **Pathos**

The final persuasion strategy laid out by Aristotle was pathos, the Greek word for 'experience'. You've seen the word pathos before, just in its modern forms. These are the words 'sympathy' and 'empathy'. By 'pathos', Aristotle meant the experience you create that leads to persuasion. In other words, the context that you set and the emotions you get your audience to feel.

BEING EMOTIONALLY PERSUASIVE

In this section, we're going to focus on the pathos; the emotional experience you create and use to persuade your audience to change their beliefs in favor of yours. Remember, nothing we've looked at so far should be done by itself. You need to incorporate all of the skills and techniques we've covered in every conversation.

The next skill to add to your repertoire is to master the art of persuading through engaging the emotional response of your audience. Let's go over how exactly you can do so.

Tell a Story

All humans have a powerful response to a great story. It's built into our brains, into our psyche, to enjoy hearing someone weave a tale of successes and failures, adventures and revelations. There are even some who say that we humans are nothing more than storytelling animals (check out the book 'The Storytelling Animal' by Jonathan Gottschall to find out more about this). When we listen to a good story, we become emotionally invested in what the person has to say. When this happens, your audience is primed for persuasion.

Make Use of Figurative Language

Linked to telling a good story is to use similes and metaphors during your conversations and debates. A simile is when we compare one thing to another using words like 'like' or 'as...as'. This can help to draw connections between what you're saying and something the audience is familiar with and, hopefully, feels strongly for or about. Think of similes that would bring to life an interesting connection in your audience's mind.

A metaphor is when we equate one thing to something else. "Time is money," for example, or, "the world's a stage." Even, "the eyes are the window to the soul," is a metaphor. We use metaphors to once again spark off an interesting connection in your audience's mind, to provide more color or clarity for your argument point, or to highlight a strong similarity between two different ideas.

Both similes and metaphors are great ways to get emotional responses from your audience and are a lot quicker to use than telling a whole story. Although, for the ultimate effect, you should use similes and metaphors inside of your stories.

Be Personal

The next step to becoming more emotionally persuasive is to be as personal as you can be. This is not only in terms of how you speak and present yourself, but also in terms of what you've got to say. There's nothing that closes the gap between you and your audience more than when you get vulnerable in front of them. For most people, being vulnerable and open can feel akin to getting naked in front of someone, but if you can get comfortable with brazenly baring all, you'll have a powerful emotional persuasion skill under your proverbial belt. To share your own experiences and open up during a conversation encourages your audience to do exactly the same.

Being personal isn't something that you can fake, and you shouldn't need to. All you've got to do is be passionate about what you believe in. Let your audience know your hopes and dreams and draw links between your argument points and your lived experience that gave root to them. Add this to active listening and setting the context and you're onto a persuasive formula for winning every argument, as well as for winning people over to your side.

6

NEURO-LINGUISTIC
PROGRAMMING

With your background knowledge complete, you are now ready to take your conversation game to the next level with neuro-linguistic programming. We've touched on a few topics that fall under the heading of 'neuro-linguistics', such as body language, active listening, and setting the context, but now's the time to get under the hood and see what really makes a conversation tick.

In this chapter, we're going to cover the history and uncover the mystery that is neuro-linguistic programming; the way that you talk to others and yourself and how it affects the context of the conversation and its outcome. Using the techniques we're about to cover, you'll not only become a master communicator, but also learn how to talk to yourself using language that empowers you to change unwanted habits, rid yourself of limiting beliefs, and become a goal-oriented, driven person. All the successful people of the world are doing it, so why not you? Read on to find out how, but first, a lil' bit of history.

THE ORIGINS OF NLP

Neuro-linguistic programming is a combination of psychology and linguistics. Which makes sense, considering that it was a psychologist and a linguist who first thought up the field of study now known as 'NLP'. It was the early 1970s, in Santa Cruz, California, when Richard Bandler, a psychology student, started to talk to John Grinder, associate professor of linguistics at UC Santa Cruz, about how some people seemed to fit the label of 'successful person', while others did not. Bandler, who had begun his studies majoring in math and computer science, approached it from a formulaic angle; they were typing in the right code. Grinder brought a more linguistic-based approach and looked at it from a language point-of-view. Soon, the two reached the conclusion that language, and how the successful people used it, was fundamentally and startlingly different to their less successful brothers and sisters. While successful people used language that encouraged themselves and everyone else, the less successful did not. Very soon, the two were so invested that Bandler left behind the world of math and computer science and changed his degree to behavioral science (which he would later get his PhD in). The psychologist and the linguist set to work creating their theory, growing it from language successful people use into a field of techniques and practices used to influence thoughts, tap into feelings, and change behaviors, both for yourself and for others.

Bandler and Grinder began looking into methods and techniques from various branches of psychotherapy ('talk therapy'). They were particularly interested in gestalt therapy, which is a branch of psychotherapy that focuses on the present life and current needs of the patient, rather than bringing up their past experiences and traumas. It places focus on understanding the context of what a person is going through and the challenges they're facing. Bandler and Grinder continued to grow and form their theory and the practice that accompanied it. They studied the language patterns used by effective therapists and read up on the techniques behind their skill, adding this to their growing database used to create NLP.

Bandler and Grinder titled their first book on neuro linguistic programming *The Structure of Magic*. The main focus of the book was to identify the language patterns of renowned and effective therapists. As they developed the theory of NLP, Bandler and Grinder began to branch out, adding to NLP with parts from the theory of medical or therapeutic hypnotism, especially that of psychiatrist Milton H. Erickson. They included Erickson's techniques for conversational hypnosis in their growing set of principles and techniques that were soon to emerge as neuro-linguistic programming.

Alongside that, they added the theories and structure of Noam Chomsky, the renowned linguist and cognitive scientist who developed transformational grammar, to form a steadfast crossover between psychology and linguistics known as 'NLP'. Since then, many others have tried out the techniques and practices of NLP and have become life-long devotees to the theory. Today, the field of NLP has grown wide and prosperous, with many different people writing, researching, and contributing to the NLP community. One that you are soon to enter, too! With the origin story told, it's now time to move on to...

STARTER TECHNIQUES FOR NLP

As we've seen, neuro linguistic programming is about how we communicate, both with other people and with ourselves. It also analyzes the way we communicate and the effect it has on the way you and your audience behave. Finally, NLP is used to influence people's emotional and behavioral outcomes (the way we feel and act). Beyond that, NLP will also help to increase your self-confidence and self-awareness, as well as greatly enhance your communication skills. It's also an extension of, or next step to, separating the map from the territory and setting the context of the conversation, as we covered back in Chapter 3. Let's go over the main beginner techniques of this fascinating field of study. Soon, you'll be such a wizard with words that nobody will be able to resist your charm nor overcome your conversational prowess.

Build Rapport

If we have good rapport with someone, we have a close and friendly relationship with them. We understand one another's concerns and respect each other's feelings. This allows for the usual social barriers to be lowered, resulting in a smoother flow of thoughts and ideas. This is the type of relationship we have with our family (the ones we're on good terms with) and our close friends. When we're around such people, there's not only a free-flow of conversation, but we also tend to take on the mannerisms and phrasing that we associate with that person or group of people. This is 'rapport', a vital skill for anyone looking to win every argument and piss people off in the right way, and yes, building rapport is indeed a skill that can be learned. You can't fake years, decades even, of memories, but you can activate your audience's feelings of familiarity and aim them toward you. To do this, we use two NLP techniques: Mirroring and matching.

Mirroring and Matching

Although it may not feel like it to some, we humans are very similar in many different ways. The way we move, act, sound, gesture, even think, is determined by the way that those around us move, act, sound, gesture and think. This isn't the case for everyone, just those stuck confusing the map for the territory. You can use this to your advantage by mimicking or mirroring their gestures, posture, facial expressions, sitting position, and even cursing words. By doing this, you can make the other person feel like you are familiar, and they will then start treating you like someone who is from the same 'area' as them.

Begin by observing and make sure not to overdo it or you'll make it obvious that you're trying to copy their body language. Before you begin mirroring in a conversation, begin by observing the way that closer friends mirror one another when chatting. See how often they mirrored each other, how long after the action the mirroring occurred, and whether it was reciprocated by the other side at any time. Once you have observed how and how often people mirror each other, take it out and test it. Try to consciously control your mirroring and matching of your close friends and family. Once you've got the hang of that, test it out with complete strangers.

You can also get very specific with the way that you mirror the other person or match their movements. You can, for example, mirror their blinking speed or match their tone of voice. Mirroring and matching work wonders, all the way up until anger is involved. If someone is downright pissed with you, then mirroring their anger is not going to do you any favors in winning that argument. In fact, it's probably going to get you a black eye at the least. In the case that you find yourself face-to-face with an angry human, remain calm, take a neutral stance, and focus more on logic and argumentation than on emotion or persuasion. That's if they're angry with you. If they're angry with someone or something else, then you can mirror their hand gestures and definitely bank on emotion and persuasion to get the job done.

Get Meta

One of the catchwords of the 21st century, 'meta' means to show awareness of oneself or to be self-referential (refer to yourself in the third-person, for example). This makes getting meta a great addition to separating the map from the territory and for setting the context of the conversation. There are two NLP techniques based on getting meta. They are:

Meta Positioning

Meta positioning means taking the point of view that we just talked about above. Imagine yourself in a position just above and outside of your current one. Claiming this vantage point, what would you see? How would you feel about the current argument point or debate topic if you were removed from the emotional shell that is your body? This is a kind of dissociation technique that allows you to analyze things from a much more logical, less emotional perspective. After you have done that, ask a question based on your meta-positioned thoughts and pose it to your conversation partner or to the group. You could also take the 'position' of your argument partner or a member of the audience and view things from their perspective. Formulate a question based on your meta-positioning and ask it before providing the answer. For example:

"You may be wondering X, Y, and Z. Well, you see, A, B, C."

Taking this kind of meta position helps us to gain more insights and see different approaches to a situation. In other words, it helps us to separate our mental map from the territory that is the conversation.

Meta Modeling

Linked to meta positioning is meta modeling. Where the former has to do with taking a third-person viewpoint or a different perspective to a conversation, meta modeling has to do with building a 'model' of yourself or the person you are conversing with. When creating your model of the person, don't focus on taking their position, but rather focus on what you perceive to be the model of them that agrees with your point of view. Then, mind-map out a way to get from A (reality) to B (your model).

Modeling

The next NLP skill to add to your repertoire is modeling. This technique is similar to the meta modeling that we just looked at but is more focused on copying someone else rather than creating a meta-model of them. Since we now all agree that the map is not the territory, why not constantly add to our mental maps?

If you see a mannerism or gesture that you like, model it and add it to your repertoire. Doing this is the same as when you hear or read some thought point, opinion, or belief, and you take it on as your own. Most people model others subconsciously. Those that know a thing or two about NLP bring this into the conscious world as they continuously add to and update their mental maps. Let's go through the three phases of modeling.

Phase 1: Observe

The first step to successfully replicating something is to find someone to use as a model. It's preferable to find someone in person, although this isn't always possible. Movies are also a great source to use. John Grinder calls this "finding your genius", in terms of finding someone who is a 'genius' at what you're trying to do. Once you've found this person, imagine what it's like to view things from their point of view. Imagine what they do, how they do it, and why they do it. These three questions cover the behavior, thought processes, and supporting beliefs of your model. Once you understand this, you have all the background info you need to move onto phase 2.

Phase 2: Practice Until You Can Teach It

The best way to know something properly is to teach it. Being a teacher is quite the thing. You have to know everything (or, at least, know how to look like you do), going from beginner, through to advanced, and then back again as you teach what you learned. Take on this mindset, practicing until you can teach what you're trying to learn to someone else with the confidence that you'll seem like a 'teacher' and not some guy doing bad impressions on the street. Remember that rehearsal is a key part of modeling, whichever way we define the word. Model away like you're learning some new dance move, for that's what it is, in the verbal dance we call a conversation.

Six-Step Reframing

The final NLP beginner skill that we're going to look at is the six-step reframe technique. This has to do with rewiring our behaviors through reframing our motives. One of the core NLP presuppositions is that every behavior we have and response we make has an intent. What this means is that our motives, what we believe in, drives our behaviors and how we act. As we grow up, we try out many different attitudes and behaviors, keeping some and discarding others as easily as we would change our style of clothing. But, as we get older, our fashion sense solidifies, as do our beliefs and behaviors. Not so for the NLP initiate though! Let me show you how to use motive to break free from the ruts of habit and complacency.

Identify

The first step of reframing is to identify the specific behavior, gesture, mannerism, or belief that you want to change. Really focus in, analyzing it from all angles and tracking it back to its roots. Make a mind map to visualize the behavioral pattern and identify the specific parts that you want to change. Think about why you want to change it and how it will make your life better once it has changed.

Communicate Your Intent

Once you have identified and analyzed the behavior or response you want to change, the next step is to visualize it and 'communicate' your intent. Close your eyes and consciously try to focus on the unwanted behavior, or alternatively, meditate on your mind map of it. Connect with it and communicate your positive intent, or will, for it to change.

Focus on the Positive

While it's sad to say, many people in this world focus more on the negatives than they do on the positives.

This is especially true when it comes to the way they view and talk to themselves, but this is not the way of the person wise to the teachings of neuro-linguistic programming. I'm sure we've all heard a quote like, "What you put out to the universe is what you get," or something along those lines, but what if I told you that this is true; it does happen. Only, it's not the universe that's doing it, but our own brains. Have you heard of the Law of Attraction before? We're not going to get too much into it here, but the basic philosophy of the Law of Attraction is that positive thinking ushers in a positive reality. As such, if you want to make a lasting positive change to a behavior or response, focus on the positive of what the benefits will be once you perfect it, not on the negative of analyzing the unwanted behavior or getting down because of how crappy you are at the new response when first testing it out. Center on the silver lining and watch it soon bloom into full sunshine.

Once you have identified the positives of the change that you're making, use these as the fuel for your intent to make the change. There are few things more powerful in the world than someone driven by a positive intention. If you live by the way of positive intent, you'll seem to brighten up the room just through the presence of your personality. And, if you present yourself this way, no matter how heated or negative the other side of the argument gets, you'll soon become their silver lining, priming them for changing their thoughts or beliefs. It's also a great technique for winning arguments with panache and pissing people off the right way. As Monty Python says: "Always look on the bright side of life!"

Get Creative

Once you have identified the unwanted behavior or response and communicated your positive intent, the next step is to access your creative side and think of all the great functions and uses of your brand-new behavior. One great way to activate your creative brain? Mind map it out! Put your positive intent into words and place it in the central circle. Then, think of all the possibilities this new behavior will have on your performance, how it will help you, and when and where you can use it. Also, list out at least three ways you can start using your intended change straight away. Just through the act of visualizing this new behavior and imagining its multitude of possibilities, you are accessing your creative mind and improving your chances of ingraining the new response in your daily life quickfast.

Evaluate and Create a Link to the Future

A key part of this NLP technique is to evaluate your progress in utilizing the intended change. This evaluation needs to be done with a focus on positive progress, not negative lack of improvement, as well as be carried out as objectively as possible. Emotion doesn't help with this unless it's linked to your positive intent. Linking your present actions to achieving a future goal is known as 'future pacing'. Set some measurable milestones of your progress along the route, evaluate, reflect, and adapt your plan according to your progress. This is how those who know about NLP learn and manage to adopt a new mannerism or gesture as easily as someone learning a new skill in their sport.

Monitor for Knock-On Effects

Once you have practiced and perfected the new behavior or response you were reframing for, the final thing to do is to monitor the ecology of your behavior for any knock-on effects that this newly updated or upgraded response has on the rest of your system. If you change something in a natural environment or computer code, it's going to have knock-on effects throughout the system. It's the same with the human mind and body. So, monitor yourself for changes in your behavior, and if the knock-on effect doesn't sit well with the new you, go back to step 2 and get reframing!

With the six-step reframing technique outlined and defined, we come to the end of this chapter on the basics of neuro-linguistic programming. Master these techniques and you'll start to gain more and more control of your mind, allowing you to separate the map from the territory and set the context of the conversation. In the next chapter, we're going to go a bit more in-depth into an important concept of NLP that we touched on briefly in this chapter: Reframing.

7

IN THROUGH THE OUT DOOR

Reframing, the art of separating the map frame the territory, is a useful and frequently used practice in NLP. Our minds are continuously framing and reframing our representations of reality based on the information coming in and the way we choose to interpret it, both consciously and subconsciously. As we saw when we learned about mind mapping, whenever we think of something, we automatically link related ideas to it and place it in the tangled web of a map that is our understanding of reality.

In this chapter, we're going to outline the magic of reframing before covering three techniques—Content Reframe, Context Reframe, and Outer Framing. Once armed with these techniques, you'll be able to see the bigger picture of how to potentially reframe any discussion, topic, or notion that you choose!

THE MAGIC OF REFRAMING

Whenever we think about something, we always put it into some frame of reference. Without framing what we think, we wouldn't be able to think about things at all. When we frame a thought or idea, we put it into a certain category; defining what it means and associating it to other similar or related thoughts or ideas we've had in the past. We also take into account the frame of reference that is our current surroundings and a multitude of other factors that add up to the average person's view of reality.

At its core, reframing has to do with changing the way we think about something and to begin using a different frame of reference or reference structure. In the previous chapter, we covered the six-step process of how we reframe our own thoughts, but it's also possible to reframe the thoughts of others during a conversation. Even if you manage to do this ever so slightly, you've won. If you can provide your audience with a new frame of reference during a conversation, link it to something they already believe in, and show how it's beneficial for them to see things from this new frame of reference, you're onto a winner.

The Seven Directions of Reframing

If we think of the great reframers of the past century, we're thinking of people like Steve Jobs, Elon Musk, and Oprah Winfrey. These are the pioneers who changed, or at least influenced, the frames of reference of millions of people around the world. Besides being skilled at creating something new in the world, these people are also highly skilled at articulating their ideas, framing a vivid picture of their vision, their dream, that everyone can see, understand, and reframe their own reference point accordingly. Added to this is obviously having the facts and figures, the proof and the passion, to show people the benefit of believing what you've got to say.

In order to begin framing and reframing, you need to take the point of view that nothing has meaning on its own. 'Meaning' is a human construct that determines what and how we think about something. Two people can look at an open field after the rain, with the one framing the picture with the meaning of beauty and nature, and the other framing the scenery as muddy with a chance of cow patties on the unavoidable walk back that is certain to ruin their shoes. A silly example, but one that captures the way that people can look at the same thing and live through the same experience but put different meaning to the different parts depending on how it fits in with their frame of reference.

Knowing this, the trick then becomes to find a way to connect what you've got to say to a previously existing reference point in the mental map of your audience. Let's cover seven directions, or dimensions, of reframing. This theory comes from a book by Dr. Michael Hall and Dr. Bob Bodenhamer titled: *Mind Lines: Lines for Changing Minds* (1997).

- **Deframing**

Deframing has to do with taking a piece of meaning apart, separating it from its context, and dissecting it through analysis.

- **Reframing**

As we've covered already, reframing has to do with changing the way you think or act to a new idea or action. It also has to do with reclassifying information.

- **Pre-framing**

Much like foreshadowing in a book or movie, pre-framing is where you set the context or frame of reference before sharing your perspective. An example of this would be to tell a short story at the beginning to set the tone of your point and build the scene in the mind of your audience.

- **Post-framing**

Whereas pre-framing is about establishing a perspective ahead of time, post-framing is about imagining a future perspective looking back on the action or point you're making. This allowed for a fresh viewpoint that can often offer new insights or different meanings.

- **Counter-framing**

This frame happens in the action of a debate or argument, and deals with providing counter arguments, explanations, or examples.

- **Outframing**

Outframing takes "look at the bigger picture" to heart as it deals with trying to get your audience to place a new meaning on something based on the 'grander-scale' frame you've shown them.

- **Metaphorical Framing**

The final reframing direction makes use of the power of story. In metaphorical framing, you turn your argument points and rebuttals into meaningful analogies spiced with powerful metaphors.

Using the seven directions of reframing, you can start to not only reframe the context of your own mind, but also the mental maps of those you talk to. Remember that it's not a "one-size-fits-all" kind of deal, and it's not going to be a one and done either. In fact, I recommend making a mind for each of your arguments and think about what you could say for the seven directions of reframing for each of them. Challenge yourself to consider your viewpoint from every frame of reference and consider how best to utilize that frame to get people to see this from your point of view.

Content Reframe

To put it simply, content reframe is the NLP way of saying, "Always look on the bright side of life," the core of the concept being to put a positive twist on a negative thought, belief, behavior, or event. Another name for this reframing technique is 'meaning reframe', as that's exactly what you're trying to do: Change the meaning of something negative to instead focus on creating a more positive framework based on that event. This can help you to overcome any unwanted emotions you may feel or to come to terms with events outside of your ability to control and overcome them through handling yourself right in these situations.

The meaning we put onto anything is determined by what we choose to focus our attention on. In order to reframe the meaning of a situation, you need to first begin by becoming fully aware of the behavior or response that you want to change. Then, use the six-step reframing process we covered in the previous chapter to create the new and improved content or positive meaning. There is always more than one meaning to be attached to something, so why not choose the one with the most positive intent? This is what reframing, and the entire theory of NLP, is about: Using language, both spoken and internal, to spread positivity and improvement. Questions that fall under content reframing include: "What else could this mean?" and, "In what way could I view this as a positive?"

Believe it or not, a central assumption, or presupposi-tion even, of NLP is that every behavior and response that we have has a positive intention, a purpose. This is true for yourself and for other people, and if you think this isn't true for any of your behaviors or responses, or that they no longer fit with the present version of you, then go through the six-step process and change them.

Context Reframe

While content reframing is better used to change unwanted behaviors or negative thought patterns, context reframing is most useful in dealing with things in the moment or in helping with sensory overload. It does this through changing the way you react to certain contexts and situations. Context, in NLP terms, is the specific setting the conversation occurs in and the situations attached to it. Every meaning we attach to something is context dependent. We wouldn't wear a bikini to a business meeting or a business suit to the beach, after all!

When we talk about context reframe, we're talking about reframing the meaning we attach to something by changing the context we associate with it. This means taking someone's point or meaning and placing it into a different context that undermines its meaning or even makes it seem nonsensical. Context reframing is a great way of showing people how the meaning of something changes when you change its context. To understand the difference between content reframe and context reframe, let's look at some examples. These will also help to show these two NLP techniques in action.

'I am too needy!'

Content Reframe: How can you aim that 'neediness' of yours in a direction that benefits your day-to-day, such as needing to complete your tasks and deadlines.

Context Reframe: Compared to who? You're no drug addict, so you're doing well. Just remember to take everything in moderation, and you'll be A-okay.

'I can't stop procrastinating!'

Content Reframe: When you procrastinate, do some menial activity and turn it into a positive procrastination session. Make a list of activities to do for positive procrastination and, when you find yourself lost in a daydream or death scroll, do one of your positive procrastination activities instead.

Context Reframe: Would you procrastinate with your life? Giving away hour by hour, day by day of your life to the god of procrastination, aka death. If you can't stop procrastinating, you can't stop feeding death your most precious possession: Time.

'I always seem to focus on what could go wrong.'

Content Reframe: Trying to focus your attention on other elements besides yourself is a good start to developing empathy and heightened awareness. Make sure to balance those thoughts on what could go right so that you get the full 360-degree treatment!

Context Reframe: There are many places where this type of attention to detail is critical, such as when building a spaceship or being a detective. You have developed the skill of spotting mistakes easily but should remember this is just one skill in your repertoire, and you have many others to focus on, too.

Outframing

The final of our reframing techniques is called 'outframing', and is greatest for getting rid of, or at least detangling a bit, our limiting beliefs. The idea behind outframing is to take a step back and try to see things from a wider frame of reference. You can even take multiple 'steps back', widening the frame of reference each time. As we mentioned, this technique is great for analyzing your limiting beliefs so that you can begin detangling them from your mind. Limiting beliefs are those that hold us back and stop us from performing at our best or achieving what we could otherwise have accomplished. In the book *The Encyclopedia of Systemic NLP and New Coding,* written by NLP coaches Robert Dilts and Judith DeLozier, this process of changing our limiting beliefs is called 'Belief Outframing'. Dilts and Delozier suggest taking three different frames of reference. They are:

- First position (your point of view).
- Second position (your close friend or mentor; someone who believes in you).
- Third position (an observer able to see all the networks and systems you are a part of, the environments you influence and are influenced by, and the relationships you have within these environments).

Then, apply past, present, and future to each of the above frames to bring the total number of belief outframes to nine. Once you have reflected or meditated on each of these frames of reference for your specific limiting belief, you'll soon find it has much less of a hold on you than before. Combine this with the other NLP techniques we've covered, and you've taken the next few leaps along the path to not only winning every argument and pissing people off the right way, but also for becoming a new and improved version of yourself. In the next chapter, we're going to move on from reframing meaning to looking at meaning itself as we learn the final few NLP tools for you to become a pro context setter and a wizard with words able to change someone's beliefs in the course of one or two conversations.

8

SAY WHAT YOU MEAN, OR IS IT THE OTHER WAY ROUND?

Welcome, my argumentative king or persuasive queen, to the final chapter of our book! It's been excellent having you on board for our learning journey through the world of winning arguments and pissing people off the right way. In this final chapter, we're going to be speaking about meaning, and what the word 'meaning' really means. Know what I mean? We'll be giving it an NLP twist as we look at the link between truth and paradox and learn how to define our purpose in relation to the larger scope of the world we find our meaning from.

The meaning of 'meaning' can only be interpreted in terms of what it does to us. The meaning that we assign to something tends to be very subjective and more than a bit biased, and this is how it naturally needs to be.

What something means to us affects us physiologically, neurologically, and emotionally, but as we have seen, it's possible to change the content and the context of what something means to us, and therefore master meaning rather than letting it master us. Our next step on this path begins with a talk about truths and paradoxes.

OF PARADOX AND TRUTH

A paradox is a statement that at first seems to be contradictory or even absurd, but when further explained or analyzed, can be true. The paradox of meaning or perspective is that we need fiction in order to tell facts. Don't believe me? Let me prove it to be true. When we live through an experience, we do so through our own frame of reference, which is formed by the information our five senses are able to gather and tinted by our thoughts and beliefs. That's when we're living through the experience. Now, fast-forward to you retelling the story to someone else a day, a week, a month, a year, 10 years later. At best, you'll remember the main plot points, and your brain is going to make up the rest from whatever information is left, gluing it all together from whatever else it can find that seems to fit with your representation of reality.

Now, let's look at it from the other side, taking the perspective of the listener to this experience you had. Their ability to understand and comprehend what you're saying has to go through a gauntlet of obstacles. The first one being how skilled the person sharing the experience is at telling a story. The second being the surrounding context of the situation. The third, how well the experience being shared fits in with their own representation of reality. And so, because it's impossible to remember everything factually, and because no-one would listen to you if you did, we need fiction in order to share a factual situation.

Paradoxes and Philosophical Puzzles

What does this mean for you and your journey of winning arguments and pissing people off the right way? Definitely not that you have a free license to just make stuff up. This doesn't work, anyway, because it won't carry the same feeling as something you truly believe in, and it's all about the feels at the end of the day. What it does mean is that you should come to terms with the fact that meaning is largely subjective, and people can only see things through their representation of reality. Knowing this and knowing the argumentation, communication, conversation, and persuasion skills that you do, you are primed for telling the truth through facts intertwined with fiction and storytelling techniques.

The famous Danish physicist and Nobel Prize winner Niels Bohr once said: "The opposite of a true statement is a false statement, but the opposite of a profound truth can be another profound truth." Let's go through a few paradoxes, some of them profound truths while others are fun philosophical puzzles you can use to spice up a conversation.

The Liar

This is an age-old paradox which dates back to ancient Greece, brought to us by a seer named Epimenides. A 'seer' is someone who was supposed to have supernatural insights and to be capable of seeing into the future. Being from Crete, Epimenides once famously said, "All Cretans are liars." This gave rise to the Liar paradox. Let's say someone told you that they were lying. Said it straight out: "I am lying." If what they say is true, then they are lying, which means that what they're saying is false, but if what they told you was false, then they would be lying, which means that what they told you was true. This is a fun paradox puzzle to do with friends who enjoy the more philosophical kinds of conversations.

The Axioms of Communication

The Five Axioms of Communication is a theory created by Austrian American psychologist and psychotherapist Paul Watzlawick and forms a part of his larger theory of misunderstanding. This is based on the paradox of choosing to avoid or ignore metacommunication during a conversation. By 'metacommunication', we mean everything besides speaking. This includes facial expressions, body language, emotions, and so on. Believe it or not, many of the skills and techniques we've covered so far, as simple or obvious as they may seem after reading them, are avoided by many. This led Watzlawick to form the axioms of communication to combat this paradox. They are:

1. It's Impossible to Not Communicate

We are communicating every moment of every day. Either with other people or with ourselves. Even when we watch TV or listen to a podcast, we are communicating with this information. Silence itself is a form of communication and can be less silent than you think in terms of the messages your body is transmitting and the context of your silence.

2. Communication is About More Than the Message

All communication has at least two levels: The content level and the context level. As we covered in the previous chapter when we talked about reframing, content is what you're talking about while context is the situation and relations of the conversation topics to the lives of the speaker and listener. As such, communication is about building relationships.

3. The Communicative Process is the Perfect Feedback Loop

Have you ever found that you could explain an idea you had much better to someone else than you could when just thinking about it yourself? Having a living, breathing soundboard for our ideas is what has escalated humans to be so far at the top of the food chain that we've pretty much separated ourselves from it. This is all because of our ability to communicate. As such, it should be a skill that we all aim to perfect as much as we possibly can, for not only the betterment of ourselves, but the betterment of humankind.

And that is why communication skills and techniques, like all of those covered in this book, are essential for anyone who wants to get anywhere in the world of today. As we have come to learn, it goes a lot deeper than just the words that we say and the way that we say them and is a lot more learnable and able to be developed than previously thought too. With that final thought on paradoxes and truths, and the relationship between them, we come to the end of this chapter and to the end of our journey into the world of winning arguments and pissing people off just right!

CONCLUSION

To the end we have come. What a journey it has been, taking you through the ropes and learning the lengths and breadth of winning arguments, being convincing, and using neuro-linguistic programming to get what you want while still somehow managing to piss people off in a way that makes them love you and believe in you and your ideas the more for it, too. Soon, your prowess with the spoken word and skill in presenting yourself and your argument points will seem like some kind of magic trick to those that converse with you or and debate against you.

Remember that it goes a lot further than the words you say and the way that you say it. You have to learn to read the room, as well as actively listen to your audience. You have to learn how to separate the map from the territory so that you can start reframing every conversation to a context that fits your audience's needs and your desires. It's also vital to mind-map out your argument points so that you have the information, the facts, the figures at the ready to aid you in reframing through content. Finally, take a step back and view the bigger picture because winning an argument or changing someone's mind isn't a one-time shoe-shine type of deal. It's a lifestyle that can help both you and those that you influence to live a better, more fulfilling life, and what could be better than that?

REFERENCES

Ables, K. (2023). *Walk a Mile in My Shoes*. Kim Abeles. https://kimabeles.com/walk-a-mile-in-my-shoes/#:

Adlam, C. (2015). *A short History of NLP (Neuro-Linguistic Programming)*. Www.linkedin.com. https://www.linkedin.com/pulse/short-history-nlp-neuro-linguistic-programming-chris-adlam/

Alison. (2023). *Effective Learning Strategies in NLP*. Alison.com. https://alison.com/course/effective-learning-strategies-in-neuro-linguistic-programming?utm_source=bing&utm_medium=cpc&utm_campaign=436347240&utm_content=1350202087964114&utm_term=kwd-84388782265337:loc-168&msclkid=4e67e830cae41977c4ea8c0622dce1a3

Aquino, J. (2016). *Persuasion Skills: How to Use the Power of Emotion to Influence Your Audience*. Cool Communicator. https://coolcommunicator.com/persuasion-skills-power-of-emotion/#:

Bechara, A. (2004). The role of emotion in decision-making: Evidence from neurological patients with orbitofrontal damage. *Brain and Cognition*, *55*(1), 30–40. https://doi.org/10.1016/j.bandc.2003.04.001

Bradberry, T. (2022). *Emotionally Intelligent Arguing*. TalentSmartEQ. https://www.talentsmarteq.com/articles/emotionally-intelligent-arguing/#:

Braithwaite, L. (2020). *There's a right way to piss people off*. Www.linkedin.com. https://www.linkedin.com/pulse/theres-right-way-piss-people-off-lisa-braithwaite-ma-she-her-/

Casabianca, S. (2021). *15 Cognitive Distortions to Blame for Your Negative Thinking*. Psych Central. https://psychcentral.com/lib/cognitive-distortions-negative-thinking

Cherry, K. (2023). *How to Read Body Language and Facial Expressions*. Verywell Mind. https://www.verywellmind.com/understand-body-language-and-facial-expressions-4147228#:

Clarke, J. (2023). *How Gestalt Therapy Works*. Verywell Mind. https://www.verywellmind.com/what-is-gestalt-therapy-4584583#SnippetTab

Clemente, S. (2022). *Paradoxical Communication: 6 Keys to Understanding it*. Exploring Your Mind. https://exploringyourmind.com/paradoxical-communication-6-keys-to-understanding-it/

Cuofano, G. (2023). *Neuro-Linguistic Programming In A Nutshell*. FourWeekMBA. https://fourweekmba.com/neuro-linguistic-programming/#:

Disabilitynorm. (2020). *(P7): The Map is Never the Territory*. Changestrategy.net. https://changestrategy.net/2020/08/24/p7-the-map-is-never-the-territory/#:

Duigan, B. (2023). *8 Philosophical Puzzles and Paradoxes*. Encyclopedia Britannica. https://www.britannica.com/list/8-philosophical-puzzles-and-paradoxes

Dunlop, M. (2014). *The Key Skills of NLP in a Nutshell*. Www.linkedin.com. https://www.linkedin.com/pulse/20141113173650-70881305-the-key-skills-of-nlp-in-a-nutshell/

Elston, T. (2019). *Eye Patterns & NLP Coaching*. NLP World. https://www.nlpworld.co.uk/nlp-coaching-eye-patterns/#:

Engaged HR. (2016). *Communication: The Importance of Context*. Engaged HR. https://engagedhr.com/the-importance-of-context/#:

Ferriss, T. (2009). *The Benefits of Pissing People Off*. The Blog of Author Tim Ferriss. https://tim.blog/2009/11/25/the-benefits-of-pissing-people-off/#:

Goldhill, O. (2015). *Keep losing arguments? A psychologist explains why emotions are more persuasive than logic*. Quartz. https://qz.com/521628/keep-losing-arguments-a-psychologist-explains-why-emotions-are-more-persuasive-than-logic#:

Goman, C. K. (2019). *Body Language of Listeners*. Global Listening Centre. https://www.globallisteningcentre.org/body-language-of-listeners/

Hall, M. (2010). *The Magic You Can Perform With Reframing*. Neuro-Semantics. https://www.neurosemantics.com/the-magic-you-can-perform-with-reframing/#:

Hypno Society. (2019). *9 Best NLP Techniques that will Help Change You Realize your Potential*. HypnoSociety.com. https://hypnosociety.com/nlp-techniques/

Landsiedl. (2023). *Six-Step Reframing*. Www.landsiedel.com. https://www.landsiedel.com/en/nlp-library/six-step-reframing.html#:

Life Enrich. (2023). *NLP Reframing - Content Reframe and Context Reframe*. NLP Practitioner Training | Hypnotherapy | Coaching | Counselling - Life Enrich. https://www.life-enrich.com/en/online-learning/nlp-reframing.html

Mandriota, M. (2021). *What Is NLP?* Psych Central. https://psychcentral.com/health/neurolinguistic-programming-nlp

NLP Education World. (2020). *How to Build a Strong Rapport using NLP Mirroring And Matching Techniques*. NLP Education World. https://nlpeducationworld.com/how-to-build-a-strong-rapport-using-nlp-mirroring-and-matching-techniques/#:

NLP Mastery. (2015). *What does context reframing mean?* Anilthomasnlp.com. https://www.anilthomasnlp.com/faq-nlp/what-does-context-reframing-mean%3F#:

NLP Mentor. (2011a). *Eye Body Language - Knowing What People are Thinking*. NLP Mentor. https://nlp-mentor.com/eye-body-language/

NLP Mentor. (2011b). *NLP Modeling, finding the structure of excellence*. NLP Mentor. https://nlp-mentor.com/nlp-modeling/

NLP Mentor. (2011c). *Representational Systems*. NLP Mentor. https://nlp-mentor.com/representational-systems/

NLP Mentor. (2011d). *The Map is not the Territory*. NLP Mentor. https://nlp-mentor.com/map-is-not-the-territory/#:~:text=What%20is%20NLP

NLP Mentor. (2011e, May 6). *The Six Step Reframe Technique*. NLP Mentor. https://nlp-mentor.com/six-step-reframe/

NLP Mentor. (2015). *Neuro Linguistic Programming - Changing Behavior and Thinking*. NLP Mentor. https://nlp-mentor.com/neuro-linguistic-programming/

NLP World. (2021). *NLP Context | NLP World - Glossary*. NLP World. https://www.nlpworld.co.uk/nlp-glossary/c/context-reframe/

Nordquist, R. (2018). *What Does Argumentation Mean?* ThoughtCo. https://www.thoughtco.com/what-is-argumentation-1689133

Northeastern Global News. (2017). *"If you can't explain it to a 6-year-old, you don't understand it yourself."* News @ Northeastern. https://news.northeastern.edu/2017/04/13/if-you-cant-explain-it-to-a-6-year-old-you-dont-understand-it-yourself/#:

Psychology Today. (2019). *Body Language.* Psychology Today. https://www.psychologytoday.com/us/basics/body-language

Rational Wiki. (2014). *Logical fallacy* . Rationalwiki.org. https://rationalwiki.org/wiki/Logical_fallacy

Rational Wiki. (2023). *Mistaking the map for the territory.* RationalWiki. https://rationalwiki.org/wiki/Mistaking_the_map_for_the_territory#:

Rolheiser, R. (1998). *Truth Is Found In Paradox.* Ronrolheiser.com. https://ronrolheiser.com/truth-is-found-in-paradox/#.ZEEg2PxBxD-

Ryan, R. (2021). *NLP in a Nutshell.* Rebekah Ryan. https://www.rebekahryan.com/blog/nlp-in-a-nutshell

Science of People. (2023). *Reading Body Language 101.* Science of People. https://www.scienceofpeople.com/body-language/body-language-101/

Smith, A. (2016). *Outframing - a practical NLP process for loosening limiting beliefs.* Practical NLP. https://nlppod.com/outframing/#:

Van Edwards, V. (2021). *5 Powerful Reasons Why Body Language is Important.* Science of People. https://www.scienceofpeople.com/body-language-important/

Wingfield, D. (2022a). *NLP Reframing: A Practical Guide to Content Reframe.* Www.lifecoachhub.com. https://www.lifecoachhub.com/coaching-articles/nlp-reframing-a-practical-guide-to-content-reframe-from-an-nlp-coach/120

Wingfield, D. (2022b). *NLP Reframing: A Practical Guide to Content Reframe (from an NLP coach).* Www.lifecoachhub.com. https://www.lifecoachhub.com/coaching-articles/nlp-reframing-a-practical-guide-to-content-reframe-from-an-nlp-coach/120

THE SELF CONFIDENCE EVOLUTION FOR SINGLE MEN

7 KEYS TO POWER, INFLUENCE, AND
SUCCESS. TRANSFORM YOUR
RELATIONSHIPS AND PROFESSIONAL LIFE.
IMPROVE YOUR MINDSET, PERSONALITY
AND SELF-ESTEEM

INTRODUCTION

When I was younger, I used to look at the confident, influential, self-assured men in my life and think that I'd never be able to build up the power and pure magnetism that they embodied. Self-confidence seemed like some kind of foreign language that I just couldn't understand, and self-esteem was some type of magic trick that I'd never learn. But, lucky for me, I've always had a strong character and the desire to develop my personal power. And, as we'll see later on in this book, strong men make their own luck.

Now that I've become the confident, influential, self-assured man that I used to look up to, I have developed myself from the average middle-class American into the powerful and empowered hero of my own story. I have become fluent in the language of self-confidence that used to sound so foreign to my ears. I have developed my own bag of "magic tricks" that make me seem like a god with the ladies to the uninitiated men that fall by the wayside. I have attracted opportunities and successes that have helped me to get what I want and manifest the life of my wildest dreams. And I am here now to help you to do the same.

Anyone can develop killer self-confidence, no matter how far down the power ladder you start. You just need someone to show you how; to mentor you in the ways of becoming a strong, outgoing, and intelligent personality. Without having the right keys, you'll forever remain wallowing in the pits of despair, with true confidence eluding you and the life of your dreams remaining exactly that: a dream. Let me give you the keys you need to succeed in opening the doors to the new, improved you, teaching you all that you need to know to turn your dreams into reality, and to become the man that every woman dreams of.

Through the seven keys that I give you in this book, each key representing a separate chapter, you'll open the doorways to becoming the ideal version of yourself. These powerful keys will arm you with all the ammunition you need to turn your personality into a potent weapon for success. It all begins with learning how to speak the unspoken language of self-confidence. Let's get your journey toward developing powerful self-confidence on the right road to success! Turn the page and take your first step to turning the life of your dreams into reality.

KEY 1

THINGS ARE NOT WHAT THEY SEEM

What if I told you that things aren't always as they seem? I know, I know, a bit cliché…how about I put it another way. Your failure to become the confident, powerful, man-about-town of every woman's wildest dreams isn't based on your own short-comings. It's because you focus on them. A lot of the time, your lack of self-confidence is the result of you being so caught up on what brings you down (what you're bad at) that you forget to tell people about what picks you up (what you're good at). In other words, you're looking at reality through the wrong lens. And, because we can't see into your brain, the rest of the world assumes that lens you show to be who you are.

Knowing this, would you be willing to change the way you see the world? I guarantee that this is how to change the way the world sees and treats you. And, before you think this is some kind of Jedi mind trick beyond your abilities, let me set the record straight. Anyone can develop self-confidence, transforming their personal relationships and professional life beyond what they ever thought was possible. All it takes is opening your mind to the possibility, learning from someone who has gone through their own self-confidence evolution (a.k.a. me), and unlearning much of what you've been taught about social and personal relationships.

There are countless misconceptions out there on how to gain power in your personal and professional life that are just plain wrong. Much of what we have been taught or thought true about the way that social and personal relations work is, in fact, false. How to really become successful in relationships and in life is so out of the ballpark from what we traditionally thought that it can be seen to be the complete opposite. That's because our traditional knowledge on desire is the opposite of what occurs in reality. The truth, as it turns out, can be more counterintuitive, intriguing, exciting, and even controversial than you ever could have thought. Things definitely aren't what they once seemed.

In this chapter, we're going to have a look under the hood of your self-confidence vehicle to see how the machine really runs. After analyzing some of the latest breakthroughs in evolutionary psychology and research into the paradoxical nature of relationships, you'll have a much better idea of the power you have to make things seem like you want them to, and how to make people see you the way you want them to, too. This is the first step to revving up your self-confidence and turning you into a lean, mean, charismatic machine. After giving you the juicy details of how desire works in the human engine, we'll then begin work providing you with the tools needed to keep any motor running. This includes learning to speak the "unspoken language" of desire and desirability, the importance of having a clear picture of what you really want out of life, love, and lust, and how to become the ideal version of you. Let's get started on priming your self-confidence vehicle to win any race you can imagine! But first, a little note on how important self-confidence is, not only for the single man, but for the entire human gene pool.

SELF-CONFIDENCE PROPAGATES...LITERALLY!

As much as we may want to ignore or deny it, we humans are animals. We might be the ruling lifeform of this planet of ours and score top-spot on the food chain, but, at the end of the day, we remain a part of Earth's grand circle of life. We still have to breathe, eat, and pass on our genes to the next generation to ensure our continued survival. And, like all animals, we don't want to pass on weak or undesirable traits down our evolutionary ladder. It's always the peacocks with the brightest and showiest feathers that score the peahens, and it's always the men with self-confidence in themselves and their ability to provide a good life for their partner that scores the ladies and make them babies. Like the band Bloodhound Gang said in their song *The Bad Touch:* "You and me baby ain't nothin' but mammals, so let's do it like they do it on the Discovery Channel."

A bit m0re of a credible source than the Bloodhound Gang for showing that self-confidence is not only desirable, but is an evolutionary trait of mankind, comes from the world of evolutionary psychology.

The Evolution of Desire

Using Charles Darwin's theory of natural selection as their base, evolutionary psychologists examine the history of human behavior and the way our brains are hardwired. They do this to show that any behavior stopping someone from getting lucky isn't likely to last long in the human gene pool, as these peeps will have fewer kids than those with the desirable traits. 'Then why do some ladies go for such douchebags?' I hear you asking. Well, this is where evolutionary psychology gets a bit controversial, and is also where things, once again, are not always what they seem. Being a douchebag isn't necessarily an undesirable trait, especially if said douche is seen as being able to protect his lady and provide for his family. Even if he just talks a good game and convinces her that he can do these things. Once she lets him stick it in and his swimmer takes hold, with that baby popping out nine months later, his genes have been passed on. As unfortunate as this is for humanity as a whole, we can't deny that it doesn't happen. Does this mean that all men should be total A-holes? No! Definitely not. But understanding this situation can go a long way to telling you why nice guys with low self-esteem finish last. As evolutionary psychologist David Buss says in his breakthrough book *The Evolution of Desire*: "In selecting a mate, women must identify and correctly evaluate the cues that signal whether a man indeed possesses a particular [behavior or] resource."

That's a lot of pressure on the ladies, especially because they can't see inside of your mind to determine whether or not you're really a good fella or not when they're choosing their mate and doing their bit to keep humanity alive. A lot of the time, all they have to go on is their own intuition and how confidently the guy presents himself to her and to society at large. So, if you're a single man with a winning personality but low self-confidence, read this book! Take the lessons I teach you to heart and use them to improve the way you view yourself and how society views you. This will not only improve your influence amongst friends and colleagues, and overall success in life, but will also increase your desirability and get you laid. Don't let the douchebags win; learn the tricks to developing killer self-confidence and help to make the human gene pool that little bit better. Now, onto our first lesson: how to recognize and use the unspoken language of self-presentation and your body.

THE UNSPOKEN LANGUAGES

If you are trying to improve your confidence and self-esteem, then you should start by looking at yourself and the way that you present yourself to the world. In other words, you should analyze your body language. Developing confidence in your body language changes the way people view and feel about you when you're in their company, and is one of the main ways to succeed in coming out on top in conversations, flirting, and in life. In this section, we'll go over what positive body language is and how it is different from non-confident body language. We'll define and refine this unspoken language of the body and help you to become fluent in not only reading others better, but controlling the confident image that you want to present to the world. Your body speaks volumes to your self-confidence, so let me teach you how to listen to it, and how to ensure people listen to you the way you want them to.

Reading and Speaking Body Language

Just like all other types of language, body language is about communicating with other people. It just does this in a nonverbal (unspoken) way that takes place at exactly the same time as the words that we say. The best way to think about body language is as a mirror to your inner emotional state that tells the person you're talking to way more about what you're feeling than your words ever could. In fact, experts in the study of body language reckon that around 60-65% of all communication takes place nonverbally. Crazy, right?

What's even crazier is that most people aren't even aware of the type of body language that they're putting out there! And it goes well beyond just the movements you make with your body.

Communication is a two-way street, which means that it takes recognizing and picking up on the body language of the other person to become properly fluent at this unspoken form of communication. From awkward silences to picking up the subtle signs of sexual tension; you've got to know not only how to present your body, but how to listen to what the person you're talking to or woman you're flirting with is saying with theirs, too. Most men don't have a clue as to what message their body language is communicating, while the majority of women are acutely aware of these vital cues. If you want to succeed in your quest of developing self-confidence and personal power, start with reading and speaking the language of the body. Let's have a look at some nonverbal communication signals that you can use to present yourself and interpret the way others feel about you.

Facial Expressions

The first body language technique for you to master is that of facial expressions. Our faces are the most animated parts of our bodies, and we can convey an entire story just with the emotions we carry on our faces. Have a smile on your dial? Then you are happy, are showing that you like the person that you are talking to, or approve of what they are saying. Frowning and unable to turn it upside down? Then you are depressed or unhappy, don't like the person that you're talking to, or disapprove of what they're saying. People, especially women, will try to interpret your facial expressions to see if they match up with what you're saying. This is because, for most people, it's easier to manipulate their words than it is to control the emotions that show on their faces. Facial expressions are a more accurate read of what our true feelings are in any given situation, as well as provide insights to what our internal state of mind is.

How can this help you to develop your self-confidence? Well, first of all, through becoming aware of the unspoken language of facial expressions, you'll be able to read people a lot better and figure out what they're feeling and thinking about you beyond what they say with their words. But, more importantly, as you become aware of your own facial expressions, you'll be able to control what emotions you let cross your face. This is key to making people view you the way you want them to, and to begin changing the way you view yourself, too. Research into facial expressions shows that the act of smiling alone is a superpower for spreading happiness, both for the people around you, and for yourself. To convey friendliness, trustworthiness, and confidence with your facial expression, you want to don a slight smile, and raise your eyebrows slightly as you're chatting or flirting with someone.

The Eyes

As the "windows to the soul" your eyes reveal a ton of info about what you are feeling and thinking. If you are uncomfortable with making eye contact, you need to practice this skill. Not being able to meet and match someone's gaze is taken as a clear sign that you are uncomfortable in their presence or unconfident in yourself. But, you don't want to glare too deep or for too long into someone's eyes, or they're going to think you're some kind of sociopath or psychopath. It's a bit of a balancing act, but a general rule of thumb is that you should meet someone's gaze until you can determine what color their eyes are. Here are a few things to think about when working on sending out the right signals with your eyes:

- **Eye Contact**

When two people gaze directly into each other's eyes, it shows that they are interested in each other, involved in the conversation, and are paying attention to what the other person is saying. But, as mentioned above, don't be creepy about it. Too much eye contact can make the other person feel threatened, while breaking eye contact or frequently looking away makes you seem distracted at best, untrustworthy at worst.

- **Blinking**

Linked to eye contact is blinking. Too much blinking and you appear uncomfortable or distressed. Too little blinking and you're thinking about eye contact too much and should chill out a bit. Self-confidence is about being cool, after all.

- **Pupil Size**

One of the most subtle of the nonverbal communication signals is that of dilated pupils. Also called "bedroom eyes", dilated pupils can show that someone is interested in you or even aroused by your company. Just don't glare into their eyes to determine this. Maintain eye contact until you can make out the person's eye color, glance whimsically into the middle distance, and then hold eye contact again until you can see if their pupils are dilated or not. If you can perfect this trick for keeping the right amount of eye contact, you'll have made yourself much more confident in the eyes of whoever you are talking to which, in turn, will help you to improve your own self-confidence that little bit more.

- **The Mouth**

As we already mentioned above, smiling is one of the best—and easiest—ways for you to show people that you are a happy and confident person. Besides that, there are a few other body language signals that you should know about related to the mouth and lips:

- **Pursed Lips**

Pursed lips, tightened lips, or a pout, is a sign of dislike, disapproval, or even a sign that the person doesn't trust you.

- **Biting Your Lips**

Although someone biting their bottom lip when you're flirting with them is a great indicator that they're attracted to you, habitual lip biting is not such a good thing. When someone bites their lips outside of intense flirting situations, it means that they are either anxious, worried, or pretty stressed out.

- **Covering Your Mouth**

One body language signal that you definitely don't want to put out there is covering your mouth. Mouth covering is done when someone wants to hide an emotional reaction that they have. At best, to hide a smile, at worst, to hide a smirk. But, who knows because their hand is covering their mouth!

- **Slightly Turned Up or Slightly Turned Down**

When a person's mouth is slightly turned up, it's a sign that they're in a happy mood or feeling optimistic. If the mouth is slightly turned down, then the person is feeling sad, or is disapproving of the situation. These changes can be slight, and so it may take a bit of practice to pick up. If you're flirting, feel free to change up eye contact by looking at the person's lips to further indicate that you're interested in them. Keeping your mouth slightly turned up is also a part of developing confident body language!

- **Hand Gestures**

Much more obvious of an unspoken language than the turning up or down of the mouth are hand gestures. It's impossible to talk without using your hands in some way. Try it, if you don't believe me, but be aware that you'll creep out the person you're talking to if you don't use hand gestures while talking to them. So, practice on someone safe. Some cultures, like Italians and New Yorkers, are much more talkative with their hands than others, but all people gesticulate and speak with their five-fingered appendages in one way or another. Our brains automatically involve our hands in conversations to help and convey emphasis, thoughts, and even our emotional states. And, most of the time, people don't even realize that they're sending out these signals with their porky pointers. Let's have a look at some of the main hand gestures for you to master if you're to become fluent at reading and speaking the language of the body:

- **Touch**

Touch is one of the most powerful ways that we communicate with others. It's the first language that we learn when we're babies, and is the first sense that we humans develop. More than that, how you touch someone is a great revealer of how you feel about them. Just don't be creepy about it. To convey familiarity or fondness, make sure to use your full palms. Don't use just your fingertips, because this can mean that you're feeling uncomfortable.

- **Palms Up or Down**

The next hand gesture for you to add to your body language repertoire for self-confidence has to do with your palms. If you have your palms up and open, you're sending out the signal that you have nothing to hide. This is because you're showing the world that you aren't concealing anything; nothing hidden up your sleeves. If you combine open palms with raising your arms, this is a great signal of acceptance, of welcoming, and of trustworthiness.

Having your palms always down when talking to someone is a signal that you're closing yourself off or are feeling defensive. But, if you use downward palms occasionally to emphasize a point you made, this is a signal of confidence, and shows that you know what you're talking about. Nobody said learning body language was going to be easy! But follow my tips and we'll have you fluent in no time. One final point about palms down is that, if you want to show someone you're not going to budge on a point, then downward palms with straight fingers is the way to go. Combine this with a quick chopping action, and you've made clear that you really disagree with what was just said.

- **Clenching Fists and Pointing Fingers**

While clenching your fists is generally a signal that you're unhappy or angry with someone or something, it can also be a sign of resolve in the right circumstances, such as when you want to show you're unyielding. Clenched fists where you have tucked your thumb inside indicates discomfort or anxiety, and should be avoided if you are to portray an air of confidence.

On the other hand, pointing your finger at someone is an authoritative, imposing gesture. If someone points their finger at you while chatting, it's not a good sign and can mean that they are talking down at you. Parents, for example, do the point to their children when reprimanding them, as do teachers to their students. Like a clenched fist, the point is generally a confrontational gesture. However, context is a big factor when it comes to body language, and playfully pointing your finger at someone with a cheeky wink added can be interpreted as a sign of acknowledging a friend or of showing approval with a point. Nothing in body language happens in isolation!

- **The Handshake**

One of the most well-known, and well studied, forms of nonverbal communication is the handshake. A firm, but not too overpowering, handshake when greeting someone instantly tells them that you are confident in both yourself and in talking to other people. Don't overdo it though, as too strong or tight of a handshake makes it seem like you are trying to intimidate or get one-up over the other person. Practice the art of giving a firm but comfortable handshake and you'll help people to feel less threatened when talking to you, as well as more willing to engage with what you're saying.

- **Hand Positions**

Where we place our hands while speaking to someone says a lot about what type of message we're trying to convey. Remember that body language hardly ever takes part in isolation, but rather happens at the same time as our verbal communication. The words that we say, how we say them, and the way that we move and use our bodies while saying them, or listening to someone else, work together to create the full picture of the conversation. With that lil' reminder, let's now learn how to read the next part of our body language related to the hands: where you position them.

- **Hands Behind Your Back**

Clasping your hands behind your back is another sign of confidence. This is because you are exposing your 'vital' parts and the front of your torso to the world in a clear indication that you're not feeling the need to defend yourself in this situation. While the general rule of thumb is to always show your hands with open palms (to show that you've got nothing to hide), having your hands behind your back can be seen as the exception to this rule.

- **Hands On Your Heart**

By placing one of your hands over your heart while speaking, you signal that you are being sincere. This doesn't always mean honesty, but communicates that you want the person to believe what you're saying "comes from the heart" and is, therefore, true.

- **Hands in Your Pockets**

Although you might think you're being cool when digging your hands into your pockets during a conversation, it can have a negative effect on your body language. This is because, by hiding your hands away, you've removed some crucial signallers from the conversation, leading the other person to have to rely more on your words and less on your body language to interpret what you're really trying to say. Hands in pockets is a sign of unwillingness or a reluctance to open up, or even mistrust.

- **Hands on Your Hips**

When combined with a negative facial expression such as a frown, having your hands on your hips can be seen as a sign of unfriendliness. But, when used in the context of work or some other activity, having your hands on your hips is a way to convey that you are ready for action, or that you are an authority on the subject matter at hand.

- **Hand Movements**

We're almost done talking about the talkies of nonverbal communication that are our hands. In this final section, we'll go over the hand movements for you to use and look out for when reading and speaking the language of the body.

- **Rubbing Your Hands Together**

Have you ever looked at people just before their food arrives at a restaurant? If you have, you'll probably have noticed that most of them begin rubbing their hands together as the waiter places their meal on the table. This is because the body language of hand rubbing is a sign of anticipation.

- **Clasping or Squeezing Your Hands**

While rubbing your open hands together is a sign of relishing something that is about to happen, clasping or squeezing your hands and closing them in on each other is a signal that you are uncomfortable bordering on nervous or even full-blown fearful. Linked to this is rubbing at your wrist or interweaving your fingers. Steer clear of these types of hand movements, as they're a clear signal of unconfidence.

- **Steepling Your Fingers**

When you move your palms to face each other with only your fingertips touching each other, this is called steepling. I've saved my best for last, because this is one of the best (and easiest) ways for you to start practicing sending out the signal that you are confident and self-assured. I've included it in the hand movements section for a reason, though. You don't want to overdo this show of power, otherwise you might make the other person feel like you are too confident for them!

- **Posture and Personal Space**

We're onto our final section of what to look out for when reading and speaking the language of the body. So far, we've covered specific body parts and how they affect your nonverbal communication signals that you're putting out there, knowingly or not. Now, we're going to cover the way that you carry your body as a whole, and the way that you place yourself compared to other bodies. When you support your body well by having good posture, you don't just look more powerful to other people, but feel stronger in yourself. So, make sure to stand up straight with hips and shoulders in line and head up, and watch your mindset improve even in stressful situations. Once we're done with covering your posture and how close you should stand to other people, you'll have all the basics of body language that you need to read others better and make them see you as a more self-assured, powerful communicator. Let's get your show on the road to successful self-confidence!

• Open and Closed Postures

By posture, we mean the way that we hold and carry our bodies. Is your body conveying confidence and openness, or boredom and submissiveness? If you adopt what we call an open posture, this means that you keep your back straight and the trunk of your body (your torso or central region where all the vitals are) open and exposed. This posture is a signal of friendliness, confidence, and a willingness to listen. If you're more inclined to a closed posture, which involves hiding the trunk of your body behind crossed arms or legs or by hunching over, then you're giving off the message of unfriendliness, anxiety, or even straight-up hostility. While standing and talking to someone, you can also widen your stance. This is known as a power position and can serve as a confidence boost to you and make you seem more confident to the person listening to you.

• Social Distancing

A phrase that has been popularized by the Covid-19 pandemic is that of social distancing. But, it was in use in body language long before the virus changed some of our social rules. The more comfortable you are with taking up space when talking to someone, the more confident you'll appear. And, the more willing two people are to stand close to one another when chatting, the more intimate their relationship is. There are four different categories of social distancing that you can use in nonverbal communication. They are:

- **Intimate Distance (6-18 inches):** Occurs during intimate contacts such as when you hug someone, whisper to them, or touch them.
- **Personal Distance (1.5-4 feet):** This is for family members or close friends. If you can stand close to someone while talking, then your relationship is considered to have high levels of intimacy.
- **Social Distance (4-12 feet):** This is for acquaintances. The closer you stand, the more familiar and comfortable you are with the person.
- **Public Distance (12-25 feet):** This is used in public speaking situations, such as giving a lecture in front of a class or a presentation at work. In these situations, more of a gap between the speaker and the audience creates a sense of authority and confidence for the speaker, but too much of a gap and you lose the intimacy of the event feeling like a conversation.

And there you have it. The basics of body language outlined and defined for you to use to become a more effective, powerful, and confident communicator today! By putting into practice the different techniques that we covered above, you'll not only change the way that others see you, but the way that you see yourself, too. Now that we've covered nonverbal communication using the body and unpacked the ways to read and speak it fluently, it's time to move onto the next unspoken language that you'll need to understand for success in relationships with the fairer sex. Buckle up, lads, because it's time to learn about the world of the female psyche.

Reading the Female Psyche

Learning how to read and speak the language of the body is a great way to increase your power, influence, and success in everyday conversations and help you to create a mindset of confidence in your personal and professional life. To improve your chances of romantic success, you're going to need more than this, though. You're going to need to have an insight as to how the female mind works and develop ways to read the subtle signs she gives off. People, especially women, are going to test your worthiness in life. This is particularly true if you're looking to enter theirs. And, most of the time, they're going to want to conduct these tests quickly, sometimes even ruthlessly. To learn how to get past this initial 'wall' that they present you with, you're going to need to learn some techniques. In this section, we'll look at some of the top tips I can give you from my experience that will aid you in your pursuit of reading the unspoken language of the female psyche.

Women Are Mind Readers

While this might not be 100% the case, it will help you a lot in the pursuit of lust and love to think of women as being able to read your mind. Or, your surface thoughts, at least. Research into the neurochemical make-up of the female brain has shown that women are biologically hard-wired with intuition. This means that they don't need to be conscious of the tells you are knowingly or unknowingly putting out there, but can rely on their instincts to read you like an open book. This is because women are the ones tasked with spawning the next generation of little humans. They have to choose their mate carefully to ensure that they are a) getting the best genes out of the bang, and b) are banging a man that will look after them during their pregnancy and help take care of their offspring after.

As we covered above, verbal communication alone is not a reliable tell of what a person is really saying, and so evolution has gifted women with an innate ability to pick up on the unspoken language of the male psyche. Men, however, have to learn about the female psyche the hard way. Realize that women are turned on by power, influence, and self-confidence (because these are good traits of a successful mate). Develop the body language for these traits, and your success at attracting the fairer sex will improve drastically.

Ladies Dislike Conflict, But Detest Not Getting a Response

Let's face it, unless you're slightly crazy, you're going to dislike getting into conflicts with other people. It's built into our evolutionary code to avoid conflict at all costs, if we can avoid it. This is because it's good for your own self-preservation to do so. Now, we all know that most men are more rowdy than women, with some women even getting turned on by a man's willingness to fight, especially if it's for or over her. But, women themselves really don't like to bring unnecessary conflict into their lives. However, one thing that they hate more than anything is not getting a response from you at all. Many women consider the "silent treatment" to be the worst punishment they can deliver to their spouse or children, because, in their minds, this is the worst treatment that they can receive. So, make sure to speak up rather than keep quiet, even if it feels uncomfortable for the conflict it causes. In the long term, it does you way better than that blank expression or long silence.

She's Easily Turned Off

We men are pretty simple creatures when it comes to revving our engines for sex. Most of the time, it only takes a woman entering our space or talking to us for us to feel that we're ready to get down and dirty with her. For women, however, it takes a bit more work, especially if you know her already and she's not just after a one-night-stand. For example, as far as a man's concerned, foreplay is the few minutes before sex. For women, however, foreplay can include everything that happened up to 24 hours before letting you in. So, if you're looking to get lucky with someone that you know, keep in mind to build a good foundation for the event rather than just hoping that it happens.

And, if you think you'll get her into bed just by being nice and friendly, think again, my friend. The saying "nice guys finish last" doesn't exist for nothing. If you're too sweet, needy, flattering, or servile, this is actually a big turn-off for women as they will start to look down on you. Just like women prefer tall men, they also prefer to look up to a man rather than down upon him. How can you ensure that you gain the upper hand on this? You don't have to be unnecessarily mean to women, but rather back off a little and show that you are a strong, self-confident man worthy of her admiration.

Speaking the Language of Goals

The final unspoken language that we'll be learning about in this chapter is that of knowing what you want. As we've seen, there's a lot more happening in the background of communication than just the words that we say. And other people, especially women, rely on these background vibes that you're giving off to prove the worth of your words. There's no point in speaking a good game if your body language shows that you don't believe in what you're saying. Bravado and swagger will only get you so far in life and relationships. To get the full benefits of self-confidence and become the influential, powerful man that you dream of being, you need to know what you want and how to get it. In other words, you need to learn to speak the language of being a goal-getter.

If you are a passive participant in your own life, then it doesn't matter how well you can read other people, because society will still decide what you want for you. Having a clear idea of what you want out of life can make the difference between achieving true happiness and feeling empty or unsatisfied with every relationship that you have, whether it be personal or professional. Let's have a look at some of the main things for you to think about when learning to speak, and live, the language of goals.

Consistency is Key

While your drive, enthusiasm, and determination for getting something are important parts of setting and achieving your goals, they all come in second to consistency. Consistency refers to your ability to repeat the same behavior over and over again until you live it. It's how well you can show up, day after day, come rain or shine, in pursuit of getting what you want out of life. When you decide what you want out of life, you'll have loads of energy to achieve it at the beginning. But, as the freshness or newness of the goal wears off, your energy to achieve it will diminish. This is where most people's drive will steer slowly but surely towards inaction. Don't be like most people. Focus more on consistency than anything else and, slowly but surely, you'll develop your fluency in speaking the language of your goals. Trust me, people pick up on your power and positive energy if you're consistently living the life of your dreams, especially if you're showing up day after day to achieve it.

To become consistent in achieving your goals, begin by writing them down and deciding which ones you're going to work on first, next, then, etc. After that, work out how much time you can spend per day or per week in pursuing this specific goal. Be realistic with this time frame, because you don't want to make it unrealistic or risk burning out after a few weeks. Remember: it's got to be realistic if you're going to be able to be consistent. Consistency is about taking one small step at a time, one after another, without stopping. Repeating one small action toward achieving your goal, day after day, requires less energy from you at once, but will provide you with better and bigger results over a longer period of time. If your goal is to become more confident in talking to people, for example, don't go out once and try to speak to as many people as you can. Rather, go out often and speak to at least one person. This is a much better key for building self-confidence and successfully achieving your goals.

Make Your Goals Fulfilling

A fact of life is that we work way harder at getting the things that we enjoy doing. If you want it badly enough, you'll make a plan to get it, and remain motivated and driven until you achieve it. And, if you're working toward something that you are passionate about, this will shine through in every aspect of your body language. Doing something that fulfills you will develop your competence and give you purpose.

Focusing on what you are competent at and improving on what gives your life purpose will leave you satisfied and increase your self-confidence. Especially if you are consistent about it. That's why fulfillment is the second part of speaking the language of goals.

Method Your Way to Success

The final tip for speaking the language of goals is to create your own framework for success. Having some kind of methodology or system in place for tracking your goal achievements will keep you consistent and driven on your journey to living a fulfilling life and increasing your confidence. To structure your goals the right way, you first need to choose the right tools. These tools will help to support you by making you more productive and your goals more digestible. It will also help you to manage your time better, reduce stress, and allow you to track your successes to keep your morale and motivation at its prime. Let's go over a few tools that you can use to method your way to success and become fluent at the language of goals.

1. Make an Organized To-Do List

One of the first things you should do when working on your goals is to write them down. Under each goal, write down everything that you'll need to accomplish in order to achieve it. Try to break down any big tasks into bite-size chunks, because this makes them much more manageable, and you are much less likely to give up at the get-go because it seems like too much work. Once you've broken down your goal into manageable chunks of to-do activities, organize them into what you need to do first, next, then, and after that. And make sure to review your progress on the regular, physically checking or crossing off any of the tasks that you've done.

You can go old-school with your to-do list and write it out on a piece of paper, or you can make use of one of the many to-do apps out there, such as *Todoist* or *Basecamp*.

2. Think SMART

By thinking SMART, I mean defining your goals in a way that is specific, measurable, achievable, relevant, and time-based. Once you've written down your goal and listed out the different things you'll need to accomplish to achieve it, make sure that it is, in fact, possible for you to achieve it. We should always stretch our ambitions when setting our goals, but there's nothing more threatening to your newfound confidence than setting the bar too high. It doesn't mean that you shouldn't reach for the stars, but it does mean that you should keep grounded in reality while doing this. Enter thinking SMART. Take the goal you wrote down, as well as all of the to-do activities for it, and run it through the SMART formula. Ask yourself:

- Is this goal or step as *specific* as I can make it?
- How am I going to *measure* my progress and know when I've improved?
- Am I able to *achieve* this with my current skills, or will I need to learn something new?
- Is this goal or step really *relevant* to my overall life plan?
- What *time-frame* am I going to set myself to achieve this goal or step?

Once again, you can write this all down if you want to, but there are plenty of apps out there that can keep you better focused on the task at hand and primed for success. Some apps I can recommend are *Goal Buddy* and *Lifetick*.

3. Reward Yourself for Making Progress

The final piece of advice I can give you for goal-setting is to reward yourself for the progress that you make. This will kickstart the feel-good chemicals in the brain and make you more likely to keep on keeping on. Soon, you'll have developed a habit of achieving your goals because it feels good to do so. Also, don't be too hard on yourself if you aren't making the progress that you thought you would, especially at the beginning. Negativity gets us nowhere in life. Rather, take it as a sign that you need to review your plan or break the task at hand into a smaller, more digestible chunk. And, once more, celebrate every step forward that you make. It means that you have become better than the day before. Foster this kind of mindset and watch your self-confidence evolve.

Speaking of evolving self-confidence, that's exactly what we'll be speaking about in the next chapter. Let's crack on with breaking you out of your negative thought spirals or cycles of fear and show you the way to get what you want out of life, as well as what the ladies want out of you if you're to put yourself in them.

KEY 2

EVOLUTION OF SELF-CONFIDENCE

I f you still think that self-confidence is some kind of ineffable art form, or some mythical thing reserved for other people and not for you, don't worry. Because this chapter is here to show you just how wrong you are. As we covered in the previous chapter when we spoke about evolutionary psychology and the survival of the fittest, self-confidence is a trait that humans, especially men, developed to ensure that the best possible genes got passed down our evolutionary chain. It's also the thing that women throughout human history have used to determine on the fly if a guy is worth procreating with.

Although we humans may have tried to separate ourselves from nature as much as we possibly can, many of our behaviors are still by-products of our biology and evolutionary psychology. This means that personal power, the laws of attraction, and even the life choices that we make aren't arbitrary, but can be defined and determined by the sciences through the study of the evolution of self-confidence in us *Homo sapiens*. If we don't take this into account we're missing out, and the entire world of human behavior will remain a mystery to us. But, never fear! Because that's why you're reading this book, and that's why I'm here to help you.

In this chapter, we'll go over fear and other "limiting beliefs" and show you the ways to change these into "how to's" for developing success and increasing your personal power. After that, we'll go over the three main ways that humans think, covering the logical, emotional, and physical brains to show that we're not nearly as logical creatures as we may like to believe. Once we've outlined just how emotionally driven we are, we'll go over how women see the world differently to men, and how to use this to your advantage when in the pursuit of lust or love. Finally, we'll arm you with some knowledge on how to pass the tests women set for us. By the end of this chapter, you'll be well and truly on the pathway to becoming a more effective, confident, and powerful member of the human race. Get pumped!

FROM FEAR TO "HOW TO"

We've all encountered fear in our lives before. And, for most of us, this fear has made us stop in our tracks or even give up completely. Feeling fearful is a natural human emotion that dates back to our earliest days as primates. It kicks off chemicals in our brains and makes us react to certain things with a seemingly uncontrollable emotional response. Throughout human history, fear has alerted us to dangers in our surroundings, or made us aware of potential threats to our physical or psychological well-being. It's safe to say that humans wouldn't have survived so long if it wasn't for our ability to feel fear. But, we wouldn't have evolved to the top of the food chain if these fears had stopped us dead in our tracks. As the British philosopher and logician Betrand Russell says: "To conquer fear is the beginning of wisdom."

Conquer Your Fears Through Understanding

So, how do we go about conquering our fears? Well, the first step is to understand that feeling fear is natural and has helped us to survive many real or perceived threats throughout human evolution. We feel weak at the knees and clammy in the hands as we walk to the edge of a high cliff because our bodies are telling us

"Hey, buddy, you want to be careful here. One wrong step and we're done for." Similarly, when we swim in deep water or in the open ocean, we may start to feel panicky, because our mind is saying "This is not our element, my man, and I can't tell what threats are about us so I'm going to keep us on high alert." These are real threats and if you don't feel fearful in these situations, then chances are your genes aren't going to last long.

However, because our brains are supercomputers always on overdrive trying to solve the puzzle of our existence and place in the world, we humans also suffer from perceived threats. These are things we think might happen, and get ourselves into such a spiral about them that we may become incapable of moving forward. Until we understand and deal with them, that is.

Understanding Breaks the Fear Cycle

Fear is a vicious cycle, especially when it is nothing more than a perceived threat or what we call a "limiting belief" (more on this in the next section). Our fear of something causes us to adopt a state of inaction towards it. This is because we are fearful of what might happen if we try and fail. In other words, we become afraid of moving forward through taking a risk. This inaction then leads us to fear the thing even more, because we determine the lack of progress that we've made to mean that we are incapable of conquering this fear. Not so, my man, not so.

Us humans tend to view the unknown as being a lot less safe than the known, because, well, we just don't know what's out there. If we don't take the time to understand what we fear and how to conquer it, our imaginations fill in the gaps with all the horrifying, terrible things that could be out there to keep us in our safe little comfort-zone bubbles. Don't be a bubble boy, be a frontiersman. Stop living in the world of imaginary "what-ifs" and begin working toward a world of "if that", as in "If that didn't work, then how can I improve for next time?"

Trust in yourself enough to set out into the brave new world with the ability to course correct while learning from your mistakes. This is how mankind became the top of the food chain, and is how you can break through the cycle of fear. First step: understand that your inability to overcome your perceived fears is imaginary. It's all in your mind. Fear as an emotional response is meant for stopping us from walking casually up to a lion or poking a sleeping bear, not for stopping you from asking for that raise or from approaching that babe at the bar. Recognize that perceived fear means that you are not valuing yourself enough and not trusting in your ability to learn and adapt. Most of all, though, perceived fear means that you are not willing to fail.

To break free of the fear cycle, you have to realize that failure is not the root problem. It's your unwillingness to fail that is the problem. Most academics agree that we learn more, and improve faster and further, from failing a few times than if we succeed straight away. Without being willing to fail, you'd never have learned how to walk, to talk, or even to take that diaper off. As we get older though, we become more and more adverse to taking risks out of fear of failure that we forget failing is the only way we learned anything in the first place. Breaking free from the cycle of fear takes understanding that these perceived fears are more in your mind than anywhere else, and coming to terms with the fact that failure is a natural part of the learning journey. Fostering this point of view, you'll begin to weaken the power that your limiting beliefs have over your mindset and take those first important steps forward to conquering self-doubt and developing your self-esteem.

Breaking Fear Strengthens the Confidence Cycle

To overcome your mindset of fear, you need to deconstruct your limiting beliefs. Everyone has things that they're good at and things that they're crap at. But, not everyone becomes demotivated to a state of paralysis by their fears. To overcome your perceived fears or limiting beliefs, you need to develop confidence in yourself and your abilities. As you break down your perceived fears, you'll improve your understanding of your own potential and personal power. This will increase your self-esteem and help you to break out of the fear cycle and into the cycle of sweet, sweet self-confidence, baby.

To help you do this, focus on how to accomplish something rather than on your fear of it. It all has to do with the power of your mindset and, although it won't happen overnight, you can break down your mental block, brick by brick. How badass would you feel if you turned the mental blocks of your perceived fears that previously consumed you into the bedrock of your newfound confidence? Pretty damn badass, if you ask me.

THE THREE BRAINS OF HUMAN EVOLUTION

Just like our fear of standing at the edge of a cliff, our desires, preferences, physical traits, and drives have evolved over millions of years of evolution. Only the most beneficial of genes required for continued survival of the human race were passed down through the generations. And, as we have hinted on already, it is women who have been the gatekeepers of this evolutionary process. Through deciding who they let impregnate them, women determine which genes get passed down to the next generation, and which do not.

This is why women are interested in finding out our drives, our attitudes and personality traits, the way we express ourselves through style and communication with others, as well as our physical and intellectual prowess. They're trying to decide if what we've got going on is worth passing on down the generational line in the form of kids. Now, knowing this, the question then becomes: Should we leave this as an unconscious process and let women do all of the choosing? Or, should we become aware of this unconscious process of natural selection and use it to our advantage? Because you're reading this book, I'm going to assume that it's option 2 that you've picked. Good choice.

The next key step on our journey to self-confidence and living the life of power and esteem that has previously been the stuff of your dreams is to shed some light on the way that we human beings have evolved and what traits have carried on through from generation to generation. We're going to be focusing on humankind's major evolutionary advantage: the brain. Once you have a better understanding of how the supercomputer of our minds has developed, you'll have a much clearer idea of what we humans are all about, as well as what we look for in a leader and in a lover. As we said back in Chapter 1, humans are nothing more than highly evolved, uber-intelligent animals. So, it's time to get a bit *'Discovery Channel'* up in here.

According to the world of neuroscience, there are three dominant structures to the human brain. Known as the "Triune Brain" model, it offers some key insights into the way that our brains have been hard-wired through our evolutionary development. These three 'brains' that we have are:

1. Primal or Reptilian Brain
2. Emotional or Paleomammalian Brain
3. Rational or Neomammalian Brain

Taking a little trip into the development of our brains will help us to better understand the way that we work. By understanding the way that our brains work, you'll be better equipped to deal with the often illogical thoughts that everyone has, and be better placed to mold your actions and change the way that others see and treat you into what you want them to. Buckle up, gents, because it's time to prime our brains for successful self-confidence.

Primal Brain

Also known as our reptilian brain, this is the oldest of the three brain structures to be developed. Our reptilian brain is where our most primal, survival-based, self-preserving behavior patterns come from. There are four things that our primal brains take care of, and they all begin with 'f'. They are:

- Feeding
- Fighting
- Fleeing
- Fucking

Besides that, the reptile part of our brains is where the behaviors typical to most species take place. These include self-defense or defending your family or territory, physical communication and dominance, or any actions that are socially approved or are used as ritual displays (such as the good ol' handshake or head nod). Let's take a second to talk about these socially approved actions and ritual displays. As you can see, socially approved actions, such as showing more affection for people that are part of your crew or that you like than you do to peeps that you don't like is as old as the human brain itself. Not only that, but ritual displays of dominance or subservience go so far back in human development that, for most people, it's an unspoken, unconscious form of communication.

Now, we might not live in the same world as our more primal ancestors, but the part of our brain responsible for keeping us safe from threatening circumstances or dangerous situations still acts and reacts in much the same way. The primal brain is what we use to determine if something is familiar or unfamiliar, because what we consider to be familiar is almost always considered to be safe and preferable, while we generally consider unfamiliar things to be suspicious or threatening until we've assessed them thoroughly. What does this mean? If you're trying to chat to someone new or enter a fresh social circle, you'll need to reach the hallowed grounds of familiarity as quickly as you can. Becoming a pro at reading and speaking body language will give you a serious leg-up in achieving this. Other than that, just be a positive, easy-going "cool guy" and you're sure to lure people into unknowingly letting down their primal threat-preventing barriers earlier and easier than they usually would.

Emotional Brain

The second of our three brains—the emotional brain— came into being during the early days of our evolution as mammals. It's also known as the paleomammalian brain and is linked to the way that we feel things. These feelings include the motivations that we have in life, as well as the emotions we feel when eating, searching for a partner, or parenting. The development of our emotional brains is when humans really started to step up our position on the food chain and led to us becoming the smartest animal on the planet. This is because it allowed us to develop enhanced learning capabilities through increasing our memory storage and our ability to think and behave in a more flexible way than what we see in other species. It also provided us with a way to monitor what was going on in the world versus what was going on in our own community or even our own bodies through laying the groundwork for what we now call the 'self'.

Because of its role in separating ourselves from the world around us through self-awareness, the emotional brain is also in charge of our judgment calls and sensory stimulations. This means that it helps us to separate the good from the bad, as well as being in charge of our reward circuits. Have you heard of dopamine before? Our emotional brains use this 'feel good' chemical to reinforce the things that we do that it judges are 'good' or positive. This is why we feel happy when we're eating, talking to someone that we like, having sex, or looking at our newborn child. It's also why going on dates where good food is involved is a great trick of the senses to make someone feel positively toward you very quickly. If you can associate yourself with 'feeling good' by kicking off a person's dopamine reaction, you're onto a winner. Reinforce that time and again, and the person will slowly become addicted to your sensory stimulation, because they want to get that dopamine kick and feel good. Little tricks to using the emotional brain to your advantage is to focus on the senses. Research restaurants with good food when going on a date to take advantage of the sense of taste. Get a fresh new haircut and wear fashionable clothes to take advantage of the sense of sight. Wear cologne and make sure to keep your breath minty fresh to take advantage of the sense of smell. Speak in a lower tone of voice and laugh often to take advantage of the sense of sound. And, finally, hug your date, give her a little peck on the cheek when greeting her, and hold her hand when talking or walking to take advantage of the sense of touch.

The way our brains are hardwired, we humans are much more emotionally driven than we like to let on. Logic just doesn't rev our engines in the same way, and we can have a far greater impact if we affect or interact with others through emotion or in a way that focuses on emotions or feelings. To seem more confident, powerful, and even attractive, don't shy away from the emotional part of our brains.

Rational Brain

The final of our three brains to develop is known as the rational, or neomammalian, brain. The rational brain is where our abstract thoughts take place. This is the home of foresight, hindsight, and insight; the place of our reflective processes. These rational thoughts are what truly distinguishes us and our brain from the rest of the animal kingdom. As the region that deals with our higher-order thinking, our rational brains are all about our abilities to process sensory information, analyze it, and learn from it. Our rational brains also store our memories, our reasoning capabilities, our problem solving, and our fine motor skills. In other words, it's all about figuring out what's going on in the world around us and how to best manipulate our surroundings to best suit our needs.

This is the most conscious part of our minds, and the part that makes up this crazy little thing we call reality. But, as the newest addition to the human mind, it has a lot less sway over the way we act and feel than the primal or emotional brains do. As much as we may get lost in our own stories of being a rational, logical person, our actions are often a lot less logical and a lot more irrational than we would like to believe. You can use this to your advantage when trying to reach familiarity with someone or to assert yourself in any given situation. To be a confident, powerful "man about town", you need to develop an understanding of just how primal and emotionally driven we humans are, and then add a sprinkling of rationality to that.

WHAT WOMEN WANT

With our understanding of the three brains of humankind in the bag, it's now time to turn to that question that has baffled men for ages. What exactly is it that women want in a man? As we've chatted over already, women don't want men who are always kind and subservient, because these kinds of men are seen as not being able to defend their families or stand up for their women when needed. But, on the other extreme, you definitely don't want to become emotionally, psychologically, or physically abusive toward women for any reason or a result of a situational experience. These are the worst people in the world and you will face the repercussions of your actions at some point. It's a fine balancing act between being too subservient and too dominant and, once again, we can learn a lot from the animal kingdom when it comes to the evolution of desire.

In almost every species on the planet, males are the ones to display their worth, as well as the ones to begin the courtship ritual with their prospective ladies. Think of the peacock's vibrant display of tailfeathers, or the two male reindeer locking horns in a vicious battle to determine who's more worthy and capable of leading the female herd. From peacocking, to fighting, to dancing, to gift-giving; the males of a given species have to pass some serious tests of courtship to win the attention and sexual affection of the much more picky females. While men generally focus on physical appearance when on the prowl for a suitable lady, women place a lot more value on personality, wisdom, strength, and intelligence when choosing a partner. Let's have a look at why it is that women don't just want to be picky, but have no choice but to be when deciding on which man to let all up in her.

Survival of the Fittest

The first reason why the females of a species have to be picky when selecting a mate is because of the trials of pregnancy. While for men the repercussions of having sex end almost as soon as the deed is done, for women, these few minutes of fun could result in a pregnancy lasting nine months followed by potentially having to raise the kid by themselves if the dad scarpered after the act. When women become pregnant, their bodies go through a ton of changes, and they are left much less able to defend themselves as this new life form grows inside of them and leeches their energy. This whole process is not just life-changing, but can be very life-threatening, especially in our not-too-distant past of living in the wild (a time period our three brains haven't forgotten by a long-shot). Then, even if the pregnancy reaches fruition and the little tyke pops out with both parties still alive, women then need to dedicate themselves to looking after and raising the kid. Over-all, reproducing is an extremely time-consuming process that requires a massive amount of energy on the part of women. And, although casual sex is becoming more and more common in our world as women become more able to protect themselves from getting pregnant, our brains are still hard-wired to survival on the savannahs of Africa. This is why, from an evolutionary perspective, women are biologically built to seek out the fittest, healthiest partner that they can so that they can be assured to get the best buck for their bang (i.e. an offspring that is most likely to survive and be worth the time and effort she puts into raising them).

Resourcefulness

Linked to the idea above of seeking out a mate that is the most physically fit is to choose a partner that is able to provide the best lifestyle for the woman and their kids. I'm sure you've heard the phrase 'gold digger' before to refer to chicks that hold money to be the most important thing in a relationship and end up seeking out 'sugar daddies' rather than men their own age or social class. But, did you know that this isn't a new development in humans? It goes way back. The fact is that men with more resources at their disposal are considered more capable of providing a good life for women and any kids they may have together. While men don't mind having sex with women that don't have any 'resources' besides their fit-ass bodies, women do.

What this means is that, while men don't care much about going out with someone well below their own social status, women generally want to "marry up", and seek out men above their social status. Now, there are exceptions to this (one-night stands, for example), but they're pretty few and far between when it comes to a woman selecting a man that she's willing to date or possibly marry, because it goes against their hard-wired biological make-up to not try and increase the amount of resources that they have through the person they have sex with on the regular.

Monogamy

This is also the reason why women seek out the trait of monogamy (having sex with only one partner) when they're looking to settle down with someone. Resources are a numbers game, after all, and if the guy is providing for more than one lady at a time, he has less resources to give each one individually. This is, of course, unless he's a chieftain or a Mr. Moneybags, in which case many women don't mind sharing him because he's got more than enough to go around, and some.

This is the complete opposite to the males of any species, where the men try to put their genetic name in the hat of as many females as they can in order to increase the chances of their genes being passed on. For female organisms, it's a game of quality over quantity. But, for the guys, it's definitely quantity over quality. Now, this is changing slowly but surely for us humans, as women pressurize us down the evolutionary chain toward being monogamous. But, it's still a strongly ingrained biological trait for men to feel the urge to sow their seeds as far and wide as they can, not really discriminating or even thinking much about the woman letting him all up in her.

So, if you're a man that's been in a relationship before but it ended because you couldn't stop gaping over or sleeping with other women, that's why. Or, if you've never even been able to hold a relationship because of your tendency to sleep around, this is the reason. This doesn't mean that it's excusable, or that you're given a free pass, but understanding the reason why men feel the urge to sleep around is the first step toward knowing yourself and your desires better. Once you've understood the way that we humans are hard-wired, both women and men, then you are well on the path to accepting your true self and changing the parts about you that don't give you confidence.

If a long-term, committed relationship is what you want to get from reading this book, then I suggest you first develop a commitment to improving yourself and making sure you are a fit and healthy catch capable of looking after your gal. Then, focus on courting one woman at a time until you find one that fits just right, making clear to them that you're not afraid of commitment, even if you are at the beginning (trust me, everyone is).

WHY WOMEN TEST US

Linked to the idea of what women want is that of the tests, trials, and tribulations that they put us men through seemingly, from our perspective, for no apparent reason. As we covered in the section above, women are a lot more selective than men when deciding on who to sleep with, who to date, and who to marry. A little piece of advice that I can give you right off of the bat is that you should never buy into the tests they set like some completely willing puppet. That's not what they're after (remember what we said in the previous chapter about subservience being a turn-off). Rather, you should aim to remain elusive, setting the tone that you're not going to play the game the way that they want you to, and that you're sharp enough to pick up on their tricks. It also shows that you know what's really going on between men and women, evolution-ary-wise, and that you've taken the time to be aware and conscientious enough to learn this. Whether the woman testing you is consciously aware of the fact that they're testing you in this way, or of your knowledge-able response, doesn't matter, because you'll still have passed their test with flying colors. Let's arm you with a bit more insight into why women test us and how to respond to them.

Evaluation

Women are constantly feeling the need to evaluate if they've made the right choice in a partner. They want to work out if their chosen man is attentive to her wants and needs, as well as if he's selfless and invested in them as a couple rather than as two individuals bumping uglies every night. What makes this difficult for us men is that women often want to complete these kinds of evaluations without having to ask or make clear that this is what they're doing. This is why most men hold firm to the belief that women want us to "read their minds" when they get mad at us for no apparent reason. This is not the case, though. It's more about showing that you understand their desire for you to commit to them, protect them, and even sacrifice some of your own happiness for them. The hardest part about these evaluations is that most women don't even realize that they're conducting them, but they still get angry and frustrated if their partner doesn't respond in the right way.

So, what can we do about it if women don't even know they're testing us? Just be as attentive, selfless, and invested in your actions as you can, and you'll go a long way toward increasing your own self confidence through increasing their confidence in you. And, this advice doesn't only apply to the romantic relationships we look to get into, but every relationship we form. Be attentive in your reading of both the spoken and unspoken languages that we humans put out there, and show through your actions that you're willing to invest your time and effort in forming the relationship through acting selflessly at times. But, remember, there's a difference between being selfless and being subservient, the main one being that you should never be a pushover and should always stand up for what you believe in.

Self-Confidence

After reading the above section, you might think that becoming hyper-vigilant and willing to change yourself according to how other people test you is the answer. But, I am here to tell you that it definitely is not. Understand that people are always going to be evaluating your worth in their lives (trust me, you do it all the time, too!), be aware of these tests, but don't give into them. Stand up for yourself, make clear to the person that you understand them and where they're coming from, but that you are no pushover. Not only will the person respect you more, but they'll view you as a more confident, powerful person for doing so. Women will find you far more attractive if you adopt the approach of being understanding but unmovable when it comes to accepting the bullshittery of other people and their tests.

And, there you have it. The evolution of confidence, from our most primal ancestors to the modern day. Through reading this chapter, you'll have gained an idea as to the bigger picture of self-confidence and how it really works. Remember that women, as well as society in general, are less impressed with a man who is perfectly polite and submissive than one who is slightly rough around the edges but more self-confident and decisive. But, don't forget to show that you understand, and care for, the people in your life and the relationships that you form, even if they test you sometimes. The most effective ways of thinking and behaving can be learned through experience and practice. Trial and error with added perseverance is the only way great men have achieved anything worthwhile throughout human history. Add to that discussions with your peers and betters, as well as reading books such as this, and you're onto a winner of a pathway to becoming a more effective, confident, and powerful man. Nothing in this world happens in isolation, so go out and practice the tools and tricks you've learned in this chapter today! Next, onto the different roles we play in life, and the difference between our personas and our true selves.

KEY 3

PERSONA VERSUS THE TRUE SELF

So far, we've covered how to become fluent at the unspoken language of the body, as well as how to think of self-confidence as an evolutionary advantage for mankind. Now, it's time to put those two together as we work on creating the image you put out into the world. In other words, it's time to talk about your persona. Just like we all play a variety of different roles in life, we also assume a variety of different personas. And it's often a different persona that we show people we just met versus our long-time friend.

Your persona refers to the character traits that others see in you, whether you intentionally put them out there or not. If you take the time to learn how to spot a persona someone is portraying, or to hone your own persona in a particular way, you'll become far more effective at connecting with the people you're talking to or trying to impress. This is why developing your persona is the next key step in becoming a powerful, influential, and successful man with killer self-confidence. And, if you're worried that you're putting on an image, well, you are! Fake it until you make it might be cliché, but it is true and does work. We need to embody the change we want to introduce into our lives before we can convince our minds that this is us. And the best way to embody the change you want to become, is to create a persona for it.

But, it's not all about creating some kind of idealistic image of yourself and then pretending that you are that. You need to start by knowing where in your self-confidence journey you're currently at, and differentiate what you believe to be your true self from the outer persona that you present to others. Only through arming yourself with this knowledge and awareness will you be able to create a lasting persona that serves to get you to where you want to be.

In this chapter, we'll begin by going over the personality archetypes that you can use to identify your current persona (as well as that of others), and that you can also use to create the new, improved version of you that the world sees. After covering the behaviors on personalities of the different persona archetypes, we'll then move onto the next key step of cementing in place your new persona: visualization and self-affirmations. And before you start thinking this is all a bit esoteric for you, keep this tidbit of information in mind: You become what you think about. So, let's get on with learning to think about the confident, powerful hunk of a man that you are, so that you can become exactly that!

THE 12 ARCHETYPES OF HUMAN PERSONALITIES

Through understanding personas and the archetypes of human personalities, you'll develop key insights and perspectives not only on what others are really saying or doing, but what you say and do, too. You'll be able to read what other people's underlying motives are, and better understand your own desires. Using this knowledge, you'll be able to see what others cannot. Keep in mind, though, that developing a persona should be a fun thing to do. It's like creating a role-play character of yourself that you can use to determine what your true character traits are, and decide how you want the world to view you. No-one can see the inside of your head, and if you want to portray a tough guy but are really a softy inside, go for it!

This will also make you more interesting to women, especially when you finally open up to them and let the tough guy persona fall away. They'll dig you for showing your "true self" to them while keeping your persona up for the rest of the world. It makes women feel special to be able to do this, especially if you make it clear to them that not just anyone can make you drop your persona like that. Just make sure that they can't see through your persona before the time that you open up, otherwise the game is lost. As such, you need to develop a deep understanding of what we call the 12 archetypes of human personalities, so that you can ensure you're using the personality properly and don't only have a thin veil that reveals your true self too early on.

The word 'archetype' is ancient Greek for "original pattern." The idea of the 12 archetypes was invented by the famous psychoanalyst and founder of analytical psychology, Carl Jung, who viewed them as the original personality 'patterns' of the human psyche. Jung used these 12 archetypes as a way to map out the range of basic human motivations. Because each of us generally tends to favor one of these personality archetypes at a time, you can use them to figure out what your motivation is currently based on, and how to create the persona that you want to embody. Developing a detailed understanding of how Jung's theory on the 12 archetypes works is beyond what we need in this book, because it would take more than one book to capture his whole theory. What I'm going to give you here are the bare-bones that you need to know in order to figure out what archetype you're currently putting out to the world, and which one you'd like to use for your persona. Remember that nothing is set in stone, and you are more than capable of achieving any lasting change to your confidence levels that you want. As long as you want it bad enough and arm yourself with the knowledge needed to succeed. We'll be splitting the 12 archetypes into three different overarching categories, or character types, with four archetypes in each one. These three categories are:

- Ego: Wanting to leave a mark on the world
- Soul: Discovering the mysteries of life
- Self: Seeking wholeness or connection

Let's go through these archetypes and lay out the desires, fears, and talents of each one.

Ego Archetypes

The first category of the 12 archetypes are the ones based around the ego. Now, ego has gotten a bad rap in recent times, and so let me just set the record straight before we dive into the archetypes based around it. The word 'ego' means your self-esteem or self-importance.

Too much of it, and you end up coming across as a pompous bastard. But too little of it, and you'll never reach the levels of self-confidence that you need to get anywhere in this world. We all have egos, but the people that get the most value out of theirs are those that understand it and use it in the right way. Let's crack on with those archetypes that are based on ego.

1. The Hero

The hero archetype bases their life off the belief that "where there's a will, there's a way." People that embody this form of motivation desire to prove their worth through bold actions and taking the initiative. Their goal is to improve the world through mastering a certain skill or talent, and their greatest fear is not being able to do this, or being seen as weak. While we may all want to be the hero, and we're all the heroes of our own stories, they are not perfect. If you associate yourself with the hero archetype, you should watch out for being lost to your arrogance. And, although heroes are sought after by the babes and admired by all, their need to always have a battle to fight often chases people away and leaves them living a relatively lonely life. As we can see from this first archetype, each one comes with its draws, and with its flaws. Although heroes are by their nature confident, being a hero is not always the best way to develop power in personal relationships or to improve your success.

2. The Caregiver

The next of our ego archetypes—the caregiver—is based around the idea that we should love our neighbors as we love ourselves. A caregiver's core desire or motivation is to protect and care for others, especially those in need of help. Their greatest fear is to become selfish or ungrateful for the life that they live. If you connect with the caregiver archetype, then you can increase your confidence and power through doing things for other people. Through increasing your social capital and improving how people view you, you'll naturally develop your self-confidence and personal power. Focus on your talents of compassion and being generous, but keep well aware of a caregiver's weaknesses of wanting to become a martyr or of their ease in being exploited by those they want to help.

3. The Innocent

The motto of the innocent archetype is that everyone should feel free to be themselves and enjoy their lives. The motivation of the innocent is to create a paradise on earth or, at least, in their own lives. These happy-go-lucky individuals are the evergreen optimists among us, and always have faith that things will work out just fine. But, should they be punished or, worse, be considered boring, their self-confidence can come crashing down around them. If you associate with the innocent archetype, then your goal should be to spread happiness. If you walk around with a dashing smile on your dial, and the attitude that you can charm the pants off of anyone, people will want to hang out with you, because you're fun. You'll also be able to win your way into ladies' hearts (and pants) through charisma alone. But, be prepared for people to think you're either naive or shallow, and work on ways to circumvent this when you need to show your "deeper self."

4. The Everyman

The final of the ego-based archetypes is the everyman. This kind of person views everyone as being born equal, and has a deep desire to connect with others. Their goal is to belong, and their greatest fear is to be left out or to stand out. The weakness of the everyman is that they lose themselves in their constant pursuit to please others and fit in. Rather than losing yourself trying to blend in, you should use your empathy to connect with others but not give up your virtues or what you believe in for them. This is how you develop the confident persona that the everyman can be. Remain down-to-earth, develop a steadfast moral code, and people will not only love you, but respect the shit out of you, too.

Soul Archetypes

With the ego archetypes done and dusted, it's now time to move onto the next category—the soul. We've all got one; nobody really knows what it does. What we do know, though, is that there are some people that feel the need to develop a deeper connection with their soul and other souls than most. Enter the soul archetypes. Let's go through the next four personality archetypes and see if any of them resonate with you. Remember, the archetype that you think you are at the moment doesn't determine the one that you always have to be. Part of developing a persona is to first understand what options you have out there, and then make your choice of which one you want to embody.

5. The Explorer

As you might expect, an explorer's personality is based around freedom and a distaste for being fenced in. This archetype is motivated by exploring what this world has to offer, and their confidence develops when they give themselves the freedom to figure out who they are. This is achieved through increasing their autonomy, defining their ambitions, and being true to their soul. As such, the goal of those who connect with the explorer archetype should be to whole-heartedly pursue a better, more authentic, and increasingly more fulfilling life. Getting trapped, fitting in, or feeling empty are the kryptonite for this personality type, as is aimless wandering or becoming too much of a misfit. To become powerful and successful through using the explorer archetype, you need to embrace the journey of life, revel in its experiences, and seek out new ways to keep boredom forever at bay.

6. The Artist

Also known as the creator archetype, the artist's core belief is that, if it can be imagined, then it can be done. To get the most out of this persona, you need to focus on creating things that have value. The artist's talent lies in their imaginations, and their creative uses of it. But, to be a confident version of this archetype, you'll need to have an attainable goal set in place and find your way to follow through with it, because the thing that the artist fears above mediocrity, is poor execution. The pursuit of perfectionism, or even receiving bad reviews, can often leave the artist down in the confidence dumps. It takes having a plan in place and seeing the fruits of their labors for a creative to attain self-confidence. So, if this archetype is you, or is one that you want to embody, then you need to imagine yourself as the powerful, successful, man-about-town that you know you can be. Create your own way to a confident reality as the artist of your persona.

7. The Lover

Those that associate with the lover archetype look to intimacy and personal experiences as their core desires. The greatest fear of the lover is being left alone, or remaining unwanted or unloved, while their greatest strength comes from the relationships they grow with people, both in a personal and professional sense. Their desire to always please others risks them losing their own identities in the process, and so the lovers among us should take care to be sure of who they are. They can do this through becoming both physically and emotionally strong and attractive. People dig it when the lover archetype is self-confident, and hate it when they're a mopey emotional wreck. To become a strong and successful person using the lover archetype, first you need to find and define your passion. Then, work on developing your commitment to achieving this passion. Combine this with a sense of gratitude whenever you achieve a step toward your passion, and you're on to a winner of becoming a proud and confident lover archetype.

8. The Rebel

The final of the soul archetypes is the rebel. Also known as the outlaw archetype, these kinds of people hold true to their rebellious nature by believing that rules are guidelines at best, and should be broken when they don't fit in with their worldview or ideals. Rebels find their motivation through a deep burning desire to prove people wrong, through their need for revenge, or through answering the call of revolution. With their aim to overturn the systems of the world that they consider to be unfair or flawed, the rebels embrace the outrage and outrageousness of humankind and make it their own. Their greatest fear is to be powerless or remain ineffectual in achieving change, and their greatest threat (both to themselves and others) is when they knowingly turn to crime and embrace the dark side of human existence. To become confident through the use of this personality archetype, you need to embrace the rebel's call to disrupt systems, or even destroy them when necessary. Not everyone needs to toe the line in this life; we need those that provide some shock factor. These seekers of radical freedom keep this world an interesting and exciting place to live.

Self Archetypes

The final of the archetype categories is that of the self. The self archetypes aim to connect their unconscious and conscious minds together to become as whole as any of us can get. These archetypes carry a lot of individual strength, but can be susceptible to many psychological problems, such as having low self-esteem or undermining their self-worth, if they don't manage to connect their conscious and unconsciousness together. Jung often represented the self archetype category as a circle with a dot in the middle. He did this to represent the conscious and unconscious thoughts, and the need for these kinds of people to make both whole in order to connect them together. Let's learn about the final four personality archetypes for you to add to your repertoire of personas that you can draw from.

9. The Fool

Also known as the jester or trickster archetype, this kind of person abides by the mantra of "you only live once." They gain their motivation through living in the moment and enjoying every second of it. Their greatest fear comes from being thought of as boring by others, or being bored themselves, while their weakness comes from wasting time or lacking the seriousness needed to get anything done. To gain confidence using the fool archetype, your aim should be to make everyone that you come into contact with have a great time as, like a ray of sunshine, you lighten up their world through your presence. You can achieve this through making jokes, poking fun of the seriousness of life, or through playing little personal games with people. Everyone loves to have a joker in their crew, and if you can find the right motivation to be confident, inside and out, you'll make the world a more joy-filled place to be.

10. The Magician

The magician archetype, also called the visionary, yearns to understand everything from the human psyche to the laws of the universe. Living by the code of making things happen, these kinds of people are driven by the goal of turning dreams into reality. The thing that a magician fears above all else is having to deal with the negative consequences of their actions, especially if these consequences are unintentionally caused. The weakness of this archetype is in becoming overly manipulative, both of situations and of people, which can lead them astray from their path and to become obsessed with control and power. To form the right type of confidence through the magician archetype, you'll need to develop a clear vision of what you want out of life and to live by it. Don't manipulate yourself into power-mongering just because you can. The best way to become powerful and successful is to know what you want out of life and to mold your personality around this image. Don't let the personality archetype that you are mold you into something that you don't want to be.

11. The Sage

The sage archetype represents the deep thinkers among us. It's also where mentors and scholars find their home. The sage archetype is driven by the desire to seek out knowledge and truth, believing that it is this above all else that will set them free. The sage's goal is to develop a deep understanding of the world we live in through their own intelligence and the analytic techniques available to them. These guys fear having the wool pulled over their eyes above all else, as well as being misled by others' manipulation or their own ignorance. If you connect with this archetype, or want to use it as a persona, you'll need to keep control over your pursuit of perfectionism. Rather than perfectionism paralyzing the sage into not being able or willing to act, as it does to the artist archetype, these people risk getting lost in their own wisdom or intelligence, forever thinking and never acting. To become a confident, powerful, and successful sage, you'll need to develop ways to self-reflect on all that you have accomplished in order to show that your actions are having a lasting effect in the real world.

12. The Ruler

The last archetype in the self category, and the final of the 12 personality archetypes, is the ruler. These kinds of people are driven by their never-ending need for control, and hold fast to their belief that power is the only thing that truly matters. But, they also look to spread this further than just hoard it for themselves. The end goal of the ruler archetype is to build a successful 'empire' for their family, for their business, or even for their community. Maybe even all three. Their greatest fear is being stabbed in the back or otherwise removed from power, or to give into the chaos that is always surrounding their pocket of control. The ruler archetype should watch out for becoming too authoritative, or taking on too much while not being willing to delegate some of the workload. If you want to develop a confident ruler persona, you'll need to exercise your personal power to become a leader of your people. The more love and adoration your 'followers' show you, the more confident and powerful you will become.

And there you have it, folks! Twelve of the most powerful personality archetypes for you to use when creating your brand new persona. Remember that your personality doesn't have to be set in stone, and the one that you show the world doesn't have to fully represent the way that you truly feel (although it does help). Also keep in mind that you can make use of different personas at different times, or show different people a different mask depending on how you want them to view you and what kind of response you want to get out of them. Developing your personas can be a great deal of fun, especially if done right.

YOU ARE WHAT YOU THINK

We've all heard the saying "you are what you eat" before. But, did you know that you also become what you think about most often? Some food for thought. If you want to become a successful, powerful man with killer self-confidence, then you need to think like one. Working on your persona, or personas, will definitely help you out with this, especially in the beginning. But, you will want to eventually give up wearing the mask of the personality archetype that you draw the most confidence from, and start to actually embody it. This is where things like self-affirmations and visualizing your future come into play. Through practicing these kinds of image exercises and focusing on the confident, powerful hunk that you want to become, you will, over time, become this ideal person that you want to be. Trust me, it works. It worked for me, and it can work for you too. Why? Because we are what we think. Our thoughts have power, and as soon as we become comfortable in thinking that, we quickly realize the need to stop putting ourselves down through negatively focusing on what we were in the past, and start positively focusing on what we want to be in the future.

Affirmations for Self-Confidence

To solidify the persona that you're busy creating for yourself, one of the best things you can do is to use positive affirmations. These are short sayings that back up the personality changes you're trying to embody. Not only will they help you to solidify your persona, but using positive affirmations is also one of the easiest and effective self-help tools you can add to your confidence boosting tool box.

To create positive affirmations is pretty simple. All you need to do is say the words "I am" followed by a phrase designed to make you feel good about yourself. It's important to use present tense for your affirmations, because then you are telling your mind that you are already living whatever affirmation that you use. If you use future tense, then you'll always be chasing the affirmation, but never reach it. If you use past tense, then your mind will view it as done and won't be actively focused on bringing that affirmation into the world. The trick lies with living the change you want to become in the present. That's why fake it 'till you make it does actually work, as long as you believe in what you're trying to become so fully that you end up embodying it even before you get there. Life has a funny way of making up for the gap between where you are and where you believe you deserve to be. And, one way to make it do so is through using positive affirmations. Let's give you one positive affirmation for each of the twelve archetypes we covered in the previous section.

1. **Hero**: I have the will, I know the way.
2. **Caregiver**: I am the protector and carer who everyone needs.
3. **Innocent**: I am free to be me, you are free to be you.
4. **Everyman**: I am the connector who brings everyone together.

5. **Explorer**: I have the freedom to explore who I am.
6. **Artist**: I am the creator of enduring value.
7. **Lover**: I am intimacy personified.
8. **Rebel**: I am the rule breaker holding power to account.
9. **Fool**: I live each moment in a state of pure joy.
10. **Magician**: I make my dreams come true.
11. **Sage**: I understand the world, and the world understands me.
12. **Ruler**: I am the one in control.

While these general kinds of positive affirmations are a good starting ground, you're going to want to personalize them as much as possible until your affirmation matches exactly what you're looking to achieve. Be as specific as possible, say them daily or whenever you're feeling stressed or negative, and you'll start to reflect this thought. In other words, you'll start to become what you think!

Visualization

With your positive affirmations in hand, it's now time to arm you with the second technique for becoming what you think: visualization. By visualizing your ultimate future, you create an image of not only what you could become, but what you will become. This is because you're willing it into being through building the picture of what it looks like and feels like, and then connecting it to the present moment in which you're visualizing it. A little trick with becoming what you think is that you have to make that thought as clear, crisp, and real as you possibly can. This isn't easy at first, but you'll get better and better at it with practice. And it will get you the results you seek.

Developing the skill of visualizing your future into being is used by the most confident, successful people in the world to achieve their goals and accelerate their success. It does this through making it clear to your mind what you want out of life and that you are not only motivated to achieve it, but are already living it. It's reality that needs to catch up with you, not the other way round. Visualization activates the power of our subconscious to find the way to achieve the goals, which means that all you need to consciously do is visualize! Let your subconscious supercomputer of a subconscious do all of the rest. Visualization also makes use of the law of attraction, which is a philosophy that states positive thoughts attract positive results, while negative thoughts bring about negative results. In other words, visualize a positive future for yourself and you'll find the people and situations drawn your way that you need to achieve your visual-

208 | JORDAN ELLIOTT

ized dreams. Let's go over a few tips and tricks for visualizing your path to success.

Be Specific and Sensory

If you want to visualize your way to success, power, and self-confidence, then you need to be specific about what goal you want to achieve. Define your goal, write it out in present tense, and then stick it somewhere you can see it multiple times a day, like on the fridge or next to your computer. Now comes the time to start creating this reality using the five senses of seeing, feeling, hearing, smelling, and tasting. Imagine what it looks like and feels like to live the life of your goal. Try to engage as many of your senses as possible when imagining this reality for yourself. Through building the picture of the goal using your five senses, you give it a solid form that your mind can understand and use to bring it into being.

Journal Writing and Vision Boards

As I mentioned in the point above, you're going to want to write your goal or positive affirmation down. This is because, through the act of writing things down, we are giving our thoughts a solid form, making them more real than if you just left them to roll around in your mind. If you want to go above and beyond, then I suggest that you also start keeping a journal where you track your path to obtaining your future goals today. Through journaling your self-confidence journey toward living a more successful and influential life, you are not only documenting your improvements, but are also doing a kind of "self-coaching" activity where you take all of your ideas, goals, and dreams out of your head and bring them into the real world.

Linked to journal writing is creating a vision board. On a vision board, you don't focus on the words of your aspirations, but on the images of your dream life. Through making a collage of pictures that capture the essence of the life you are visualizing for yourself, you are arming your imagination with the ammo that it needs to succeed in building the picture of your future in so much detail that your mind can't help but find ways to make it reality. You can make your vision board on a piece of paper or in the same book as your journal, on your wall, or on a poster board. I have found taking images from the internet and using an app like *Canva* or *Powerpoint* to make it into a screensaver or desktop background for my computer to be most effective, because you are sure to see that vision board every time you log on.

And there you have it. Two essential ways to begin your journey of visualizing your future into being today. But, remember that creating personas, self-affirmations, and vision boards are not the only things that you need to do. You can't just sit around passively imagining your goal and expecting it to come to you. You need to show your mind that you are actively pursuing your goals and are further confident in your ability to achieve them. This is how you turn your persona into your true self.

KEY 4

THE MIND IS MAGIC

We covered the surface of how powerful the mind is in the previous chapter when we talked about how we become what we think. Now it's time to dive on deeper as I show you how to dominate your reality. Remember that what you hold to be reality is created inside of your own mind. If you want to become the successful, confident hunk that I know you can be, then you need to believe it yourself and then tell reality that you won't take no for an answer. Our minds are unlimited in their potential to think of the most grand and glorious future image of ourselves, but can also put in place devastating self-limits that chain us down to our past. I'm here to tell you that mind over matter really works, and that what matters is how much you are able to believe in yourself and your mind's power to own your reality. To do this, you need a combination of strong beliefs and to deny your limiting thoughts the time of day.

The fact that we create our own reality isn't some mambo-jumbo pseudo-science. Look around and you'll see, humans have created and dominated this reality. Most of us just do it subconsciously and remain passive in the process. Change this. Become an active creator of your reality, focus on your desired outcome, believe in your personal power, and your mind will find a way to make it happen. This is where the true 'magic' of our world is to be found. It's been inside of each of us all along. It just takes someone coming along and pointing out what's been in front of you from the very beginning. Let me be your guide into the magic of the mind and how you can use it to develop killer self-confidence, dominate your thoughts, and create the life of your wildest dreams.

In this chapter, we'll begin by covering limiting beliefs, how to identify them and what to do about them. After that, I'll chat you through how to change your thought patterns through reframing your focus and letting go of your preconceived ideas before covering how to create a positive mindset through a combination of goals, purpose, and meaning. Then, we'll talk about how strong men create their own luck before ending off with how to own your success. After reading this chapter, you'll be well on your way to developing the skills required for attaining powerful self-confidence and turning the life of your dreams into reality. Let's get your show on the road to success!

LIMITING BELIEFS AND WHAT TO DO ABOUT THEM

We all have those thoughts and beliefs that bring us down in life. And, at first, these limiting beliefs can feel so real and cemented in place that we consider ourselves unable to take even the slightest step forward to dealing with them. Most of the time, it's only you that cements these beliefs and thought patterns into place. You give them meaning and provide them with the power to hurt you. But you can also take their power away, if you change what they mean to you. You just need to know how. And that's exactly what I'm going to show you in this section.

How to Rid Yourself of Limiting Beliefs

The first step to rid yourself of limiting beliefs is to realize how our brains connect meanings to situations and experiences, and how they create specific contexts in which these meanings are triggered. By context, I mean the underlying circumstances that are necessary to make sense of a situation or idea. Most of the time, we only have our past experiences to rely on when trying to contextualize what's going on in our lives. And if our past experience hasn't been the best, it can be difficult to break free of the belief that we're just not cut out for whatever it was that we were trying to do. This is when limiting beliefs take root. These negative states of mind affect our ability to make good decisions, to try out new opportunities, or to reach our true potential. Being stuck in such a rut of negativity often affects our entire mindset and stops us from living the life that we deserve.

Step 1: Identify

What caused your limiting belief? Was it instilled in you by your family dictating the way that you or the world should act or be? Was it something to do with your education or did it happen when someone you viewed as an authority figure put you down? Or was it brought about by a negative experience that scarred you so deeply that you began to believe that the damage was permanent? There are a ton of reasons as to why a limiting belief comes about, but it isn't always clear which one was the root cause. This is especially true if you're only identifying your limiting belief years after the fact. Here are some tips I can give you on how to properly identify the cause of your limiting belief:

1. List Out Your Beliefs

To begin with, you're going to want to make a list of all your beliefs, both positive and limiting. After you've made a nice long list of your beliefs, group them together into a bunch of different categories. These could include finances, relationships, fun, and work. Once you've listed out and categorized your beliefs, it's time to put a tick next to the ones helping you, and put a cross next to those that are limiting you.

2. Objectively Analyze Your Behavior

Other than listing out your beliefs, or adding to it, another way that you could identify limiting beliefs is through analyzing your behavior patterns. Think about the times when you've acted in a way that goes against how you would have wanted to act in that situation. Ask yourself why you acted this way, and try to do this as objectively as possible. Think of yourself as your very own science experiment in these situations, and write down, as an objective observer would, what you think the reason was for this unwanted behavior pattern.

3. Take Note of Things You Find Challenging

The final way to identify your limiting beliefs is to write down any challenges that keep cropping up in your life. These challenges are often the result of a belief you've indoctrinated into yourself as fact. Once you've identified a recurring challenge, try and match one or more of your beliefs to this challenge that could bring it about, or make you react to it in certain unwanted ways.

Step 2: Overcome

After you have successfully identified your limiting beliefs and have an idea as to what could be the root cause of it, the next step is to work on overcoming it. Limiting beliefs aren't set in stone, and you have the power within you to defeat them and bring lasting change to your life. It won't be easy, especially if this limiting belief has been stuck with you for a while, but it is possible. You just have to develop an awareness of the belief, and commit yourself to becoming the future you that has already kicked said belief's ass and moved on with his awesome life. Here are some tips for overcoming your limiting beliefs:

1. Organize Your Space

The first step to overcoming your limiting beliefs (after identifying them) is to get organized. And I don't mean in your mind this time, I mean in your environment. A tidy house is a tidier mind while a cluttered, messy place is only going to make it that much harder to concentrate and remain focused. Do yourself a favor and keep your living space as clean and organized as you can. Doing so will not only improve your ability to remain focused and committed to achieving your goal of getting rid of your limiting beliefs, but it will also improve your positive thinking and even your overall mental health. To declutter your mindset, begin by decluttering your environment.

2. Explore and Be Curious

Curiosity may have killed the cat, but a lack of curiosity definitely kills the man. If you're not willing to open your mind to the possibilities of exploring somewhere new or doing something you're curious about, then you'll become closed-minded. Closed-mindedness is a breeding ground for limiting beliefs. Break free from the couch of your comfort zone and challenge yourself by doing something completely different or unexpected. This will help to open your mind and challenge your perception of the world, and of yourself!

3. Meditate

To develop control over your limiting beliefs, you're going to need to get control over what you think. There isn't a better way to do this than through meditation. And if you're one of those people that switches off whenever they hear the word 'meditation' or the positive effects that this has, you may want to add that to your list of limiting beliefs. The end goal of meditation is to develop the skill of detaching yourself from your thoughts; to let them pass through your mind without feeling the need to engage with them. It costs you nothing except a few minutes a day to start meditating, so what do you have to lose? Sit yourself down somewhere comfortable, close your eyes, and focus on breathing in and out. That's all it takes, and I guarantee it will help you to calm the cluttered mess that is the human mind. Once you've meditated for a while, you'll be able to separate your wanted thoughts from your unwanted thoughts and start to focus on adopting the positive beliefs and changes that you want to introduce into your life.

4. Focus on Self-Improvement

One of the prime ways of overcoming any limiting beliefs that you have is to challenge yourself, body and mind. Even if the personal development you're undertaking doesn't have a direct connection to your limiting beliefs, just working on improving the person that is you can be enough to break you free from your negative thought patterns and overcome your weaknesses. Self-improvement techniques include reading books such as this one, written by authors who have the beliefs you want to introduce, as well as listening to podcasts, setting personal goals, and keeping a journal to monitor your progress. Creating an exercise routine, and sticking to it, is also key to improving yourself and developing confidence in your abilities.

5. Say Your Positive Affirmations

As we covered earlier on in this chapter, positive affirmations are a great tool to use in the pursuit of boosting your self-confidence. Through making you speak positively about yourself, these affirmations help you to break down your limiting beliefs and celebrate your strengths. Say your positive affirmations day after day, and soon you'll begin to believe them, and, before long, you'll even begin to embody them.

REFRAMING YOUR PERSPECTIVE

As we have seen so far, the mind is way more magical than we give it credit, and what we think about most often is often what we become. For most people, this means that their past experiences and the meanings they created from them determine the direction their lives go in. But, that's not the way that your life is going to go, because I'm going to tell you how to fix this. Armed with the knowledge you've learned so far in this book, you're now well on your way to becoming the confident, successful, man-about-town that we both know you can be. It's now time to add the next tool to your self-confidence repertoire: how to reframe your perspective. The most effective way to solve our self-imposed limits is to change our perceptions. Through this, we'll be able to change the meaning that we associate with situations and experiences. In other words, we need to change up our frame of reference through questioning our beliefs, values, and things that we unknowingly put negative meanings to. Let's have a look at how we can reframe our perspective to change the way we infer meaning to things that happen in our lives.

The Reframing Process

By reframing our perspective, I mean that we need to change the context you use to view the world, as well as your emotional responses to certain situations or experiences. Through doing this, you'll not only change the meaning of these events in your life, but also your ability to react to them in the way that you want to. The facts of a situation can't really be changed, but our assumptions that we knowingly or unknowingly make about them can. Changing up the way we react to something is the next key step in becoming powerful, confident, and successful. Use the personas and affirmations that we covered in the previous chapter, as well as the work we've done so far in this chapter on conquering your limiting beliefs, to enforce a new you that not only responds to the world differently, but that the world responds to differently, too. Once you have a clear image in mind of what you want to become, then it's time to get your reframing on. Here's how:

First, Know Your Present Frame

The first step in the reframing process is to develop an understanding of how you currently see the world. Take a step back and try to objectively consider how you are currently framing reality. What lenses are you looking through? Are they useful for the person that you want to be or are they keeping you blind to your true potential? What assumptions have you made up about yourself in your mind's eye? Is this the point of view of a confident, positive person or one that's holding you back from achieving what you want out of life? Try to once again think of yourself as your own science experiment, or as the greatest and most important project that you've ever undertaken. It doesn't matter what negative points come out of your analysis, because these are just indicating what you need to work on and improve. Knowing what you need to reframe isn't a bad thing. In fact, it's exactly what you need to know in order to get to step two of the reframing process, which makes it a good thing. It's all about the way that you view it.

Then, Reframe to the New You

Reframing your perspective can feel a lot like someone who never believed that they needed glasses, getting a pair and then realizing how much better, clearer, and more colorful the world around them is than they ever thought possible. This is the power of the reframe. Now that you know what persona you want to show the world, I want you to think about how this type of personality archetype views the world around them. What lenses do they use to frame their reality? How would the world look from their (now your) perspective. Close your eyes and imagine what the world looks like through the eyes of this new you. Write down the description of this new frame of reference. Next, think about the limiting beliefs that your previous frame of reference seemingly couldn't get over, and then consider how easily your new point of view would challenge and overcome these beliefs.

If we become comfortable in questioning the context of a situation, then we'll be able to change what it means to us. This is because the context that we create is often more important than the bare-boned facts of the experience itself. As we have just learned, the concept of changing contexts and beliefs can be quite simple to apply, and yet it has a powerful impact on our ways of thinking and acting. When applied in the way I described above, this reframing of your perspective will give you more personal power and control over your life. Change your frame of reference, and embrace the magic of expanding your mind to becoming a new, more confident, you.

Goals, Purpose, and Meaning

To help you with reframing to the new you and conquering your limiting beliefs, it's important to know your goals, purpose, and meaning. While many people think these terms mean the same thing, there are key differences between the three. Understanding how they are different will help us to figure out what we do, why we do it, and how we want to impact the world. Let's have a look at what each of these terms mean and how you can use them to improve your self-confidence and upgrade your frame of reference.

- **Goals**

Goals are the things that we want to achieve. Whether they are short-term or long-term, professional or personal, our goals are the specific and measurable objectives that define what we want out of life. There are heaps of different reasons for setting a goal, such as goals of losing weight or gaining muscle, of getting a girlfriend or securing that promotion. What all of our goals have in common, is that they tell ourselves and other people what we do and what we wish to do.

- **Meaning**

Our goals cover what we do or wish to achieve in life; our meaning tells us why we do it. It's the emotional impact, or significance, of what we do. We human beings are meaning-seeking and meaning-making creatures. We are always on the lookout for what we consider meaningful, and are continuously comparing experiences and situations to the meanings we have already ascribed. As such, meaning is not something that can survive on its own. We create meaning in our lives, or feel that things are meaningful and worth pursuing. As such, meaning is very much linked to our motivation, and taking the time to define what gives our lives meaning is a powerful step toward becoming a motivated goal-getter. This is a trait almost all confident people have, and is one that you'll need on your journey to becoming the more powerful, successful, meaningful man of every ladies' wildest dreams.

- **Purpose**

The final of the trio—purpose—is created through a combination of our goals and what we consider meaningful. This is because our purpose represents the impact that we want to have on the world. It's difficult to develop purpose if you don't first have a very clear idea as to what your meaningful goals in life are. So, begin by working out what you want to achieve in life (your goals), ask yourself why you want to achieve them (your meaning), and then use these answers to guide you in defining your long-term purpose. Once you've done this, you've set yourself up a feedback loop for success. From this moment on, you can use the definition you've formed of your purpose to create further goals for accomplishing what's meaningful to you. Through this, your beliefs will go from limiting to limitless.

MAKE YOUR OWN LUCK

By now, I'm sure you've begun to realize just how magic the mind really is, and how much of a mental magician you are in terms of your ability to change any undesirable thought patterns for ones that you want. Through following the steps laid out in this chapter, you'll be able to get yourself out of the downward spiral of your limiting beliefs and firmly into the new reality of the confident, successful, hunk that you are becoming. Embrace this new you, own it, and revel in the limitless power of your mind. Now, it's time to take it a step further. It's time to learn how to make your own luck.

Strong Men Make Their Own Luck

Have you noticed how some people seem to be just plain *luckier* than others? This is because a positive mindset begets positive results. As crazy as it may sound, you can attract your own luck. All it takes is having the right kind of attitude. When you internalize a positive attitude and become an optimist at heart, your mind has the power to subconsciously change not only the way that you react to the world, but also the way that the world reacts to you. Your thinking processes, your determination, and your ability to overcome any setbacks will all become changed for the better if you live your life by the motto: "The better I am, the luckier I get."

People are considered to be lucky when life just seems to work in their favor. We often think that these "lucky souls" make no effort to be lucky, it just happens. But I don't believe that this is true. It's the way that they use the magic of their minds that makes them this way. In other words, they get lucky for the sole reason that they *believe* that they are lucky. Just like a pessimist sends out sad vibes into the world and an optimist sends out happy vibes, the luckiest sends out lucky vibes into the world. And the world responds to them in the same way. So, how can you get yourself onto this lucky wavelength and start getting lucky with the ladies and in life today? Once again, the best place to start is with positive affirmations. Through telling yourself over and over again that you are always in the right place at the right time, you will start to embody this thought and give it power. Then, you will find yourself being in the right place, at the right time, and make it seem like pure luck that you ended up there. That's the trick, my friends. The lucky amongst us truly believe that they are lucky, and so life smiles on them with good luck. There are two things that lucky people do to attract good fortune. They are:

1. Be open to new experiences and possibilities; and
2. Expect good fortune to come your way

It's as simple as that. If you don't believe that you are lucky at the moment, then that's where positive affirmations come into play. Say these affirmations day after day, write them down in the present tense to give them a real form in the present, and watch your luck begin to change. Positive results lead to more positive results as far as this goes, and soon you'll realize the pure magic that our thought patterns are, as long as we whole-heartedly believe in what we want to achieve and become. Here are a few positive affirmations that you can use to get luckier in your life:

- I am blessed with the luckiest fortune.
- I always get what is best for me.
- I am open to my greatest good.
- My time to shine is right now.

Soon, you'll be living the luck factor and make it look easy while doing it. Little do people know that it was your own mental strength and determination of will that made you the lucky bugger that you are.

Own Your Success

A final word to the wise before we end this chapter on the magic of the mind: Only you care about what you want to achieve. This doesn't mean that other people don't care about you, it means that you shouldn't need to convince the ones that love you about what you want to achieve, and that if you're only trying to improve your influence and self-confidence to impress others, then you're doing it wrong. You need to own your own success, learn to trust your gut, and listen to what your intuition tells you. Make up your own mind as to what (or who) you want to go for or need to achieve, and then strive to obtain it. This is the only way to make use of the magic of the mind. Constantly aspire to improve, and you will be able to achieve the life of your dreams. Through making your dreams reality, and doing it for yourself, you will own your success. It is all for you, and you know inside why, and how, you attained it through your own merit. This is the way to obtain killer self-confidence.

KEY 5

INTERNALIZE YOUR POWER AND BELIEFS

With great power comes great responsibility. But, on the flip side of that coin, if we are responsible in the development of our inner strengths and beliefs, we can achieve great power. The strongest and healthiest of mindsets comes from developing inner strengths and beliefs. But, it's scary how few people actually think for themselves. Most of us take our cues on how to act and what to believe from those nearest and dearest to us or, even worse, from society at large. This means that the majority of people are relying on other people to determine what they think and do. This makes reality one great game of the blind leading the blind, and is the reason why many of us remain insecure in what we believe; feigning that we know what we're doing rather than really trying to figure it all out. Not for those with true self-confidence, though. Not for me, and not for you.

As with anything, to become an expert in the art of self-confidence, you first need to start by learning the fundamental truths of the way it all works, as well as cover your basics. That's what we've covered in this book so far as we learned about personality traits and the ways to communicate what we want and how to show it, both to ourselves and to others. Through these chapters, you will have discovered which tools and techniques work for you, and which strongly influence others.

When we develop and strengthen our beliefs, it shows. Through doing this, we become more in control of the persona that we adopt until it becomes the person that we are and we are comfortable in our new skin. This happens as we begin communicating through our thoughts and actions, both verbal and nonverbal, rather than through our reactions. Believe me, people can tell when we express and demonstrate who we truly are, what we want to be, and what we believe in. If you learn how to do this with confidence, the world will respond strongly to you as you begin to bring your thoughts and beliefs to fruition. Remember what we said in the previous chapter about strong men making their own luck?

In this chapter, we're going to be continuing on with our journey of developing your inner strength and arm you with the tools needed to become responsible for your own fate and fortune. We'll be learning how to talk to ourselves in such a way that grows inner strength and internalizes your personal power while ensuring that you are responsible for your own beliefs. Remember: with great responsibility comes great power.

DEVELOPING INNER STRENGTH

To begin internalizing your power and beliefs, taking your persona to the next level, you'll need to develop inner strength. This is the deeply felt and unstoppable belief that you have in yourself and your abilities. Through developing inner strength, you'll become capable of weathering any storm, and truly be the captain of your own ship. Through internalizing your power and beliefs, you'll become less dependent on the actions of others or the circumstances that surround you, and more dependable. This is the next step to developing killer self-confidence, as well as to appearing more confident to others.

Human Resources for Inner Strength

By inner strength, I'm referring to the mental and emotional resources that we have at our disposal. These include the behaviors, the skills, and the attitude that we use to get through the day and make it our own. Inner strength is what we use to successfully adapt to situations and to bounce back from any adversity that we may encounter. Let's go over what these 'resources' look like before arming you with some strategies for developing your inner strength.

Emotional Skills

Humans are emotional creatures. In fact, many people are so emotionally driven that they let their emotions take the driver's seat in their lives. To develop inner strength, you're going to need to get control over your emotions. To do this, you're going to need to practice the art of mindfulness. The University of California-Berkeley defines mindfulness as "Maintaining a moment-by-moment awareness of our thoughts, feelings, bodily sensations, and surrounding environment." Through developing mindfulness, you'll be able to better control your reactions and become more emotionally resilient. You'll also be able to internalize the positive emotions of love, self-esteem, compassion, and gratitude, as well as become more relaxed, funny, and responsible (yes, you can be all three). You'll also be able to get rid of any unneeded emotional responses that you have. These are key to developing your inner strength. We'll look at how you can become more mindful in the next section. For now, just know that your emotions don't define you; you define your emotions.

Outlook and Personality

Just like we can control our emotional responses, we can also determine our outlook on life and the personality that we use to engage with it. Having a confident, open, and determined outlook for life isn't some unknowable magic trick. It just takes learning the magic of the mind and how to use it, followed by continuously reinforcing this outlook through conscious action until you've internalized it. And, as we saw earlier in this book, a lot of internalizing the systems that you want to embody takes first knowing what they are, then learning how to reflect them, before finally becoming them. This is why personality and the persona that you show the outside world is also the basis for developing your inner strength.

Strategies for Inner Strength

Just as people aren't born with six-packs and the bodily strength of an athlete, inner strength also isn't an innate personality trait. Like your body, inner strength is developed through practice and continuous training. And, like an athlete, the way to begin is by having a coach show you the ropes. Consider me you coach, and let me continue to show you the ropes of how to develop killer self-confidence. Next up is to cover some of the strategies that you can use to grow your inner strength, realize your true potential, and unleash your personal potential. Let's go!

Develop Empowerment Rituals

To develop inner strength, you need to incorporate rituals for success into your daily routine. These rituals include saying your positive affirmations, visualizing your dream life using your five senses, recording the progress you've made in becoming your chosen persona in your journal, as well as mental and physical exercise. I recommend that you make a routine of morning and/or evening rituals, and to combine it with meditation. Meditation is the best way to become more mindful and gain control over your emotions, and it's a lot simpler to do than people think. All you need to do is sit yourself down somewhere nice and quiet where you won't be disturbed, keep your back straight, close your eyes, and focus on your breathing. Breathe in and out of your nose as slowly and deeply as you can, holding it for a few seconds when you've inhaled as deeply as you can, and for a few seconds when you've done a full exhale. And voila! You have just learned the art of meditation. Combine it with saying your positive affirmation as a kind of mantra or visualizing your ideal future as you breathe in and out, and you'll have primed your day for success. I suggest aiming for about five minutes of meditation time in the morning to start your day as the perfect way to begin introducing empowerment rituals into your life.

Become Conscious of Your Choices

The next strategy to developing inner strength is to understand that our choices define our lives. We humans are the only species on the planet that can consciously choose what we want out of life, and what kind of meaning we want to attach to certain experiences. This means that we are the ones that define our circumstances, it isn't our circumstances that define us. We might not be able to stop certain things from happening, but we are the ones that determine the ways that we deal with them. If you have true inner strength, you'll be able to face any decision head-on, and use it as an opportunity to become even stronger. How do you do this? Through taking responsibility for your own life. Remember: with great responsibility comes great power. Be the architect of your own life, and design your mind, body, and personality the way that you want it to be. This is inner strength.

Let Go of the Past

To develop inner strength, you're going to have to put the past behind you and face your future. This doesn't mean that we forget about what has happened to us, but that we don't let it hold us back or prevent us from living the life we deserve. Inner strength doesn't mean you won't get knocked on your ass at times, but that you'll always get back up again and keep going. You might not be responsible for every bad thing that has happened to you, but you are responsible for not letting it determine the rest of your life. Everyone has challenges to overcome or failures that set them back. The truly successful amongst humankind are those that don't give up. Seek out the positive meaning in failure, use it as feedback to improve for the future, and as a way to further improve your inner strength. As the self-help author, motivational speaker, and life coach Tony Robbins says: "The past does not equal the future unless you live there."

Focus on Your Future Wholeheartedly

The final strategy to develop your inner strength is to increase your ability to focus. To use another quote from the good ol' Tony Robbins: "Where focus goes, energy flows." Review your goals, meaning, and purpose that we covered in the previous chapter and add them to your daily empowerment ritual. Don't sweat the small stuff and make the conscious decision to focus on what really matters, being a goal-getter. Single-mindedly focus on achieving your goals, developing your purpose, and giving your life the meaning that you whole-heartedly desire. Focus on the future you have visualized for yourself, believe in your ability to achieve it, and any negative experiences that you have along the way become nothing but small, insignificant setbacks to your overall journey.

THE POWER OF YOUR INTERNAL DIALOGUE

As humans, we all have a voice inside of our heads narrating our lives. This voice comments on what's happening around us and how we react to it. Also known as self-talk, your internal dialogue runs all the time, both consciously and subconsciously. Most people are controlled by, some even haunted by, their internal dialogue. Those who have internalized their power and beliefs through developing inner strength are not only better able to hear their inner dialogue, but are more skilled at controlling and manipulating it.

Talking Your Way to Higher Self-esteem

As we covered in Chapter 3, you are what you think. This is because your thoughts, a.k.a. the voice inside your head, a.k.a. your internal dialogue, is you. It's a natural thing for us humans to be harsher and harder on ourselves than we are on other people, especially when things don't go according to plan in our lives. But, this harsh self-criticism is hardly ever helpful, and often has the opposite effect of motivating us. It can even be the very reason for our low levels of self-confidence in the first place. To develop self-esteem and inner strength, you're going to have to learn to talk to yourself the right way. Let's cover some techniques you can use to gain control over your internal dialogue and to develop positive self-talk.

Become Aware of Your Cognitive Distortions

To begin talking your way to higher self-esteem, you're going to want to start by becoming aware of your cognitive distortions. These are the irrational thought patterns that cause negative emotions such as depression or anxiety to take hold and rule our lives. Up until the point that we refuse to let them do so, that is. Most of the time, it's the distortion, rather than the actual situation, that is causing us emotional pain and holding us back from achieving our true potential. The first step to overcoming them is to realize this, and then to document when such negative and irrational thought patterns arise. The best way to deal with cognitive distortions is to understand what causes them to arise, and then to create positive affirmations to combat the negative thought patterns.

Become Your Own Motivator

Once you've become aware of your cognitive distortions and have formed positive affirmations to combat them, the next thing to do is to turn your internal dialogue from the infernal doubter to the eternal motivator. To develop belief in your ability to succeed is known as self-efficacy. This, along with your ability to persevere no matter the circumstances, is what you need to succeed in life, love, and the pursuit of self-confidence. This task is made a whole bunch easier if your internal dialogue is backing you to succeed rather than trying to bring you down. Every time you feel like you're slipping back into the bad habits of self-deprecation or despair, or that your internal dialogue is on the negative side, remind yourself that you've got this, that you can handle it and anything else that life throws at you, because you believe in yourself. Become your own coach, your top fan, and your most valuable asset. All packed up in one powerful package: yourself.

Work On Your Internal Tone

After defining your cognitive distortions and becoming your own motivator, the third and final thing to work on for improving your internal dialogue is to develop a tone for your inner voice that fits the improved, more confident you that you're busy manifesting. As you become more comfortable with this new way of talking to yourself, you're going to want to choose a new tone for your internal dialogue, too. Just like with actual speaking, it's not just the words that you say that matter, but also the way that you say them. This is where tone of voice comes into play, taking you beyond just listening to your internal dialogue to actually feeling the change that you are in the process of making. Choose a reassuring, self-assured tone of voice for your internal dialogue, and you'll soon start speaking to others in the same confident tone, too!

Through internalizing our power and beliefs, we become capable of achieving anything that we set our minds to. In time, inner strength will come to be a natural part of your personality and will reshape the way that you communicate with yourself and with others, as well as make you able to deal with anything that life throws at you. We've all heard the saying that failure can be one of the greatest opportunities to learn, and it's true. As long as your inner dialogue tells you that it is. You have to embrace this perspective and tell yourself that failing is often the only way that we can overcome our fears and break free of what's been holding us back and grow in a meaningful way. Doing this will, in turn, increase your inner strength and resilience, as well as your belief in your personal power, which will further solidify your positive internal dialogue and silence your inner critic. This is how you break free from the negativity of feedback loop from hell that our internal dialogue can be, and it all comes through being willing to try and fail. To get back up, and try again.

Having an unwavering belief in yourself and what you want to achieve out of life often means caring less about what others think. Knowing that you come first in your own existence and clearly defining what you want out of living are two key mindsets for success and self-confidence. They make it possible to visualize what you want and enable you to deal with anything that tries to get in your way while achieving it. Now that we've covered the inner game of your internal dialogue and internalizing your strengths and beliefs, it's time to look at how to reflect this to the outside world. Let's get our outer game face on for the next chapter!

KEY 6

THE OUTER GAME

We all play certain roles in life. These include both personal and professional roles, and are reflected in the skills we demonstrate to others, as well as through our personality traits and inner convictions. Life is the greatest game that we can possibly play, my friends, and it's a shame that so many of us don't realize this and take part. Develop confidence in your own abilities and then always look for ways to improve and reach the next level. As Sherlock Holmes says, the game is afoot, and it's up to us to solve the greatest case of our lives—how to become the best version of ourselves that we could possibly be.

In this chapter, we'll cover the importance of attitude and composure in conveying self-confidence before returning to the world of desire as we learn about the laws of attraction. After that, we'll discuss ways for you to stand out from the crowd and then add some more ammunition to your arsenal as we arm you with some "go-to's" for certain key situations. Let's take your game to the next level and show people that you know how to play with the pros, and aren't here to mess around.

LIFE IS AN RPG

Have you ever played a role-playing game before? These are games where you play the part of a character in a fictional setting, starting off as a weakling and then leveling yourself up as you explore the game world and gain new experiences or win certain battles. In almost every RPG out there, the aim is to become strong enough to overcome anything that this fictional reality can throw at you. But, take away the fictional aspects, as well as the ability to save or restart, and an RPG starts to look a lot like real life. We all have the roles that we play, the strengths and weaknesses to our character traits, and the challenges that we have to face and overcome to become stronger.

Play the Game

Viewing life like one massive RPG can help you to not only grow into the character that is you, but also to seek out ways to constantly "level up" and to face challenges head on in order to do so. It's also a lot more fun to think of reality this way. Let's go over some of the tips and tricks you can use to start thinking of life as the greatest game you could ever play.

You Are the Main Character

It's important to come to terms with the fact that you are the main character in the game of your life. But, just like you are the main character in your own life, everyone is the main character in theirs. Or should be, at least, if they're confident enough to play the game. Not only are you the main character, you're also the player who decides what this character that is you does and in what ways you level up. Don't hate the player, hate the game. Or rather, love the player and win the game. This is what comes from viewing life like one massive RPG. In the real world, your "main character's" stats are quite different to what they would be in your typical video game. In the place of leveling up to improve your abilities at fighting and killing monsters, you're leveling yourself up in ways that upgrade how well your abilities contribute to improving your personal power and your place in society.

Define Your Attributes and Skills

After you have defined your main character and worked out the way you want to play them, the next step is to work out your stats. Some common attributes you could use are strength, dexterity, constitution, wisdom, intelligence, and charisma. Strength refers to your athletic prowess, while dexterity has to do with your agility. Constitution is how hardy your resolve is, as well as how resilient your body is. Wisdom has to do with your common sense, perception, self-discipline, and empathy. Intelligence, your ability to learn, as well as to apply logic and your experiences to reason out any situation. Finally, charisma is the pure force of your personality, and is linked to how persuasive you are as well as your leadership capabilities. Give yourself a score out of 20 for each of these attributes, or a percentage out of 100 if you prefer, based on how well you can do the related skills for each of them. And, like all great games, your aim should be to get more and more skillful as you gain experience. It should also be to seek out the experiences that will provide you with the skills you want or the attributes you need to "level up."

Embrace Your Storyline

The next key part of your RPG is to develop an origin story that conveys the emotions, core virtues, attitudes, and beliefs you embody. These factors will become your 'compass' that help you to make the right decisions on your journey. And, remember, that while the experiences of your life story aren't changeable, we can change the ways that we think about them or relate to them. Use the personality archetypes that we covered earlier in this book to help you do this. Take the negative experiences that have happened to you in your life and think about how your chosen archetypal persona or character would view them. This will also help you to gain power over these negative experiences through seeing them as plot twists necessary to make the story interesting and to have leveled you up to the person that you presently are. Your story isn't over, and it will continue to develop and build up as you continue to progress in the game of life. The only way to survive and improve in this game is to continuously stand up to new challenges and use them to improve the main character that is you.

Using this approach to life, you'll find yourself developing your mindset in a different way to what you did before, even approaching the overcoming of your daily challenges or completion of your goals in a different way. Because, in this great RPG game called life, it's through these things that we reach the next level of our personal adventures.

ATTITUDE AND COMPOSURE

Now that we've covered the way to think about the "Outer Game" as one massive RPG, it's time to learn how to put your outer game-face on. This is ultimately achieved through developing the right attitude and becoming a calm, cool, and composed character that seems to be able to take anything in their stride.

The trick to confidence is to be calm and overly comfortable in any given situation. Tension and nervous ticks are behavior traits that you want to get rid of a.s.a.p., because they hurt your image and diminish your personal power. And, don't do this to try and impress others, but because you are the hero of your story and that's what heroes do. As such, do it to impress yourself, and expect other people to do the same. You are the knight in shining armor in your own story. Start acting like it. If you're not keen on playing the hero archetype, then choose one of the other eleven we covered back in Chapter 3 and choose the one you want to become as your game. Then, live that archetype with the attitude of a boss. Embody it in your body language, communicate it with the tone of your voice, and compose every aspect of your life around living this persona until you become it.

Body Language and Tone of Voice

As we covered way back in Chapter 2, the unspoken language of the body makes up 60-65% of the message that we're putting out there. If we add the tone of our voice to this, this number can increase to encompass up to 90% of what we're really trying to say. As such, it's vital for developing the right attitude and composure to master the power of communication. Because it is one of the most powerful tools that you can use, we'll be covering some more tips on how to communicate as the cool, calm, and self-confident character that you are well on your way to becoming.

Perfect Your Smile

If you only work on one thing out of your body language, then make that your smile. When you smile at someone, you automatically go up in their books. Smiling at someone makes them want to smile back, whether they are aware of that or not. As such, it makes your interaction with the person a positive exchange without you needing to say a single word. Not only this, but people are more likely to remember you more clearly when you smile, even if all they remember about you is that you had a winning smile. Finally, smiling makes you appear more trustworthy, more approachable, and makes people more likely to be open to what you've got to say.

To perfect your smile, all you need is a mirror and some patience, as well as the techniques I'm about to go over with you. If you practice these techniques, you'll be smiling like a pro in no time!

1. Smile With Your Eyes

All great smiles begin with the eyes. Through smiling not only with your mouth and lips, but also with your eyes, your entire face will beam with natural positivity as your facial muscles relax. To see whether or not you smile with your eyes, or to learn how to do so, block your mouth with the palm of your hand and then smile into the mirror. Can you see that you're smiling without needing to look at your mouth? If yes, then you're smiling with your eyes. If no, practice until you can. Like any muscle, it will take practice and regular exercise to perfect your smile and ensure that everything from your eyes to your mouth lights up when you beam your cool, calm, and confident composure to the world.

2. Take Care of Your Teeth and Lips

One of the key parts to any smile is, of course, your lips. Another is your teeth. If your lips are always chapped or inflamed, this is a major turn-off and you should invest in some lip-ice or seek some medical advice if it persists. Likewise, if your teeth are anything other than pearly white, then you should make a plan to fix this. If you are a smoker or regular coffee or wine drinker, then you should make sure to buy some teeth-whitening toothpaste or to rinse out your mouth regularly with water or mouthwash. Also, take that trip to the dentist every six months or so to have a check-up and ensure everything is A-ok with your chompers.

3. Practice Makes Perfect

As we mentioned earlier, smiling uses muscles. As such, if you're not happy with the way your smile looks at present, then get to work exercising it and molding your smile just the way you want it. Practice in your mirror and find the shape of smile that you consider perfect for you. Then, hold that smile for around 5-7 seconds, using your fingers to keep it in place if you have to. Train yourself to keep this smile in place by practicing this regularly and you'll soon have it locked

254 | JORDAN ELLIOTT

in and loaded as muscle memory. But remember to keep it looking natural!

Speak in a Lower Pitch

The tone of your voice, whether the inner one you use for your internal dialogue or the outer one you use to speak to the world, is very important in displaying a confident, composed attitude. Through lowering the pitch of your voice, you'll seem to become stronger and more reliable to people over night! Having a lower tone when speaking is seen as a trait of people in positions of authority or of men with strength and high levels of self-confidence (or testosterone). Use a lower pitch and see the ladies begin to treat you differently right away!

Nodding and Mirroring

The final piece of advice I'm going to give you on improving your body language has to do with nodding and mirroring. Now, you don't want to seem like a bobble-head or a mime, but you also don't want to seem like a brick wall. To show that you are engaged in a conversation or listening to what someone else is saying, nod. A nod shows that you understand what they are saying or that you agree with what they've just said. It also helps you to seem more natural in conversations (if not overdone). Secondly, by mirroring their facial expressions and even their posture or hand movements (once again, don't over-do it), you'll make it clear to the person that you are keeping up with their story and are interested in them and what they have to say. Mirroring is also a way to make someone like you, because they believe that you behave in similar ways. On the flip side, keep an eye out for nods from your listener when talking to someone, and see if they start mirroring your actions and facial expressions as a clear indicator that they are interested in you.

There you have it! A few more tips and tricks to add to your growing arsenal. Also keep in mind though that you want to be the one in control of the conversation if you want to be seen as having a confident attitude. We make countless judgements when meeting or speaking to someone, especially if it's for the first time. We judge their social status, their intelligence, and even their compatibility with us, often all subconsciously using the unspoken language of the body. To display your confidence, you should always be the one that is judging others for how well they fit into your world, not the one who is being judged according to how well they fit into someone else's.

ATTRACTION IS NOT A CHOICE

Attraction is not a choice, it's a mechanism. If you don't understand what that means, think back to what we covered in Chapter 1 when we talked about the evolution of desire and what we covered in Chapter 3 in terms of becoming what we think. We attract what we desire, period. As long as we are confident enough to desire it whole-heartedly. Enter the law of attraction. When first learning about this fundamental law of human behavior, it can seem a bit like learning about a computer program. Once you've learned how to send out the right commands and put out the right signals using the universal code, the law of attraction guarantees that you'll get something back close to what you desired. The more precise and defined you make the request you code out, the closer what you receive back will be to what you wanted. Through learning to manifest what you want out of life, you'll also be learning how to reprogram your brain and attract the life and people that you desire.

The Law of Attraction

Our minds are some beautifully powerful supercomputers that can help us to achieve what we want out of life, but if we've programmed them using trash thoughts, then trash is what you'll attract. If you want to manifest the life of your dreams, then you need to begin by altering your inputs and upgrade your programming by removing any thought patterns that don't fit the code of the new you. This book has helped you to do this by arming you with the knowledge you need to change your mind and become the confident, powerful, man-about-town of your dreams. Let's go over the steps you need to know to recode your mind and get the most out of the laws of attraction.

Set Your Intention

Your intent, or your purpose for achieving your goals, is the perfect place to start attracting the life that you desire. By focusing on what you want to attract, you are speaking the language of goals, and the world will listen to your intentions. It's important to keep in mind that your intentions aren't set in stone, but evolve and change as you grow bolder and stronger. Because intention is all about focus, you should only focus on one at a time, manifest it into the being that is you, and then move onto the next. Start with one that is relatively easy to achieve, and can be accomplished in a short amount of time. A few days to a week or so should be good. Begin small and then work your way up using the practice of positive affirmations that we covered earlier on in the book. Once you have achieved

258 | JORDAN ELLIOTT

one intention, move onto the next one, making each larger than the last as you get more into the practice of manifesting them. But, always try to break your larger goals into smaller, quicker, bite-sized chunks of intentions that your consciousness is able to accept as reality.

Get Your Mind On Board

The supercomputers that are our brains are the thing that separates them from all other animals on the planet. This is a plus side to being a human being, because we can come up with plans and solutions for any problem that comes our way. The down-side, however, is that we can also get so caught up with the stories of our lives and over-analyzing every part of it that our brains can end up paralyzing us into inaction as we think of reason after reason that we can't do something. To stop this from happening, focus on the future and your intention for it; don't dwell on the past. If you're trying to live by the law of attraction and manifest the reality you desire, you're going to need to get your mind on board. If you've spent a large amount of time focusing on what's going wrong with your life, then it's going to take some effort to redirect your focus and get your mind to believe in the new you. That's why you should start small and work your way up, proving to your mind that you're capable of achieving what you set out to. And, don't aim for perfection or beat yourself up when it doesn't all go according to plan. More than messing up, blaming yourself for it and reliving your failure over and over again is far more harmful to the new mindset you're trying to instill. Rather, accept that making mistakes is human and that failure is an intrical part of any learning journey. This is the way to show your mind that you are not interested in manifesting past wrongs, but are intent on attracting future successes. This is the way to get your mind on board with the change that you want to achieve.

Through setting your intention through bite-sized chunks and getting your mind on board, you'll begin reprogramming your mind to make the full use of the law of attraction. This is the way to make lasting change in your life. Combine these powerful techniques with the rest of those covered in this book, and you'll have successfully developed not only killer self-confidence, but the powerful, influential life of your dreams. I guarantee it.

KEY 7

SAY ANYTHING IN ANY WAY

Welcome to the final chapter! Here we will unravel the final key needed to expertly develop the self-confidence of a true king and to live the life of power and influence that you've only dreamt of. As we have come to see, a lot of what makes self-confidence has to do with communication. Developing killer self-confidence deals with what you say to yourself and how you say it, as well as how you communicate with others using both the spoken and unspoken languages of humankind. If you learn how to communicate the right way on these different levels and practice your skills constantly, it will become more and more subconscious and slowly but surely form into a permanent habit. Nothing worthwhile happens over night, and you may trip and stumble a few times while en route. But, through focusing on your future, visualizing the persona that you want to become, and using the law of attraction to your advantage, you'll be able to get right back up again and keep going. It's not like self-confident people don't fail at times, they just know how to use it to their advantage as a learning experience rather than as something which haunts them for life. It all comes from being able to look at life in the right way.

In this chapter, we're going to cover some final tips on how to communicate both with your subconscious and with other people in such a way that they can't help but give you what you want. Let's add a few final magic tricks to your skill set as I set you well and truly on your way to living the life of your wildest dreams.

IMAGINATION IS KEY

It's estimated that our subconscious minds are thousands of times more powerful than our conscious ones. This means that, in a battle between logic (our conscious minds) and imagination (our subconscious minds), imagination wins every time. That's why we've focused in this book on imagining your way to successful self-confidence through the use of personality archetypes, visualization techniques, and attracting what you desire through connecting with your subconscious. Understand the basic truth that imagination makes us what we are, use the techniques covered in this book, and watch all doors open for you. If you can tell yourself the story of what you want to become using the five senses to visualize exactly what this ideal version looks like, feels like, sounds like, etc., your subconscious mind can't help but put this out to the universe, and the universe can't help but attract it to you.

Now, imagine being able to influence anyone that you meet. It's not impossible, not even very difficult. All you need is to know how and then put it to practice. One of the best ways for you to do this is through your communication skills, specifically through the skill of conversational hypnosis.

CONVERSATIONAL HYPNOSIS

Through understanding the way to use conversational hypnosis, you'll be able to charm the socks off of anyone, and make it look effortless. It will arm you with the power to not only master the art of the conversation, but also to make every conversation that you have with other people seem far more meaningful and ensure that you're the one in control. And, best of all, it won't seem forced, manipulative, or coercive, because people will be having a great time whenever they're in your company. Through using the method I'm about to teach you, you'll not only get people to do what you want them to, but will make them feel good while doing it. In this way, using this technique will not only make you a better person, but make the world a more fun place to live. Let's get started.

Mindset is the Magic

As with most things in life, having the right mindset is the first step toward success. If you implement the plan that I've outlined for you so far in this book, you'll already be primely placed to develop the confident mindset and attitude required to use conversational hypnosis to full effect. You need to be able to connect with people from the first moment that you begin to interact with them. To do this, you need to have the intention of doing so, as well as know your persona inside and out. You also need to have control over your thoughts and opinions, and have a thorough understanding of how to read and speak the language of the body.

With this achieved, your next step is to sync yourself with the person you're talking to as quickly as possible. You already know yourself, now you need to focus on making the other person's life more fun and fulfilling in the short amount of time that you're talking to them.

Remember: conversational hypnosis is about hypnotizing the person you're interacting with, not yourself. In other words, it's all about them, not you. To accomplish this, it's easiest to think of every conversation like a stage performance where you're the greatest showman in the world and your only focus is on keeping people engaged and entertained. Think of your persona as your stage presence, and your personality as being larger-than-life. It helps to rehearse an arsenal of talking points beforehand so that you are prepared to fill every lull in the conversation and make it seem effortless to do so. But, make sure that it comes off as natural and not mechanical to do so. This comes through practice and knowing your 'act' in and out.

Most importantly, to develop the magical mindset needed to use conversational hypnosis, you need to treat your audience with the warmth and respect that comes from having a genuine interest in the people that you're talking to. Show appreciation for the fact that you wouldn't be able to put on your best 'show' without having an attentive audience.

Perfectly Integrate Your Thoughts and Actions

Most people can tell when you're smiling through heartbreak, or when you're trying to make others relax while feeling completely stressed out yourself. If there is too much of a difference between what you're thinking versus what you're saying and doing, people will pick up on this and your efforts at conversational hypnosis will end up in the gutter. That's why you need to fully embrace your new persona and the law of attraction in order to successfully use the magic of conversational hypnosis. Get your mind on board and make sure that you are able to focus on your audience rather than on what's going on in your head, otherwise your performance won't pack half the punch that it needs.

As the old adage goes, men can't multitask. If you're not focused on your actions because your thoughts are conflicting with what you're doing or saying, then your body language will give you away long before you have the chance to hypnotize them. You need to be in the right frame of mind *before* you begin the interaction. If you find that your head is too full of conflicting thoughts to focus on your 'performance', then you need to go back to working on your persona and refining your act. Only through this will you be able to hypnotize your audience to the greatest effect.

Constantly Find Ways to Connect to Your Audience

The next step to conversational hypnosis is to build rapport with the people you're talking to, whoever you're talking to. To build rapport with someone means that you work on reaching a state of harmony with them, understanding their feelings and ideas, and communicating with them accordingly. Find something that you have in common, like a hobby, sport, movie, or song that you both like, and use this as the crux of the conversation.

It's natural that you'll find it easier to communicate with some kinds of people, especially those with similar interests and experiences to your own, than with others. A little trick, though, is that those people who feel truly comfortable in their own skin are almost always able to find ways to connect with anyone. This is because they give off the vibes of calmness, comfortability, and security that become contagious. These are the kinds of vibes you want to put out there, and the type of personality that the more confident you have become through putting into practice what you've learned in this book. It will always be more difficult to connect with people who are awkward, withdrawn, or nervous, but it becomes pretty much impossible if you are putting out the same kind of energy, or adapting yours to meet theirs. Remember that interactions are a performance, and that you are the showmaster who determines the way that people feel when they talk to you. You have the power.

Hypnotize People With Your Stories

One thing we know about humans is that we all love a good story. The case can even be made that it is our abilities to tell and remember stories that sets us apart from all other animals and has allowed us to imagine our way to the top spot on the food chain. Stories have the power to transport us away from reality for the time that the story is being told, giving us permission to be someone else for a brief moment. To make the most out of conversational hypnosis, you'll need to develop the skill of weaving an engaging and entertaining story. Start building a repertoire of stories and rehearse them until you can deliver them with feeling and confidence. Not all stories have to come from things that have happened to you, but you do have to deliver them with a comfortable, relaxed speaking voice.

To keep people listening to your story and invested in what you're saying, you can make use of what we call power words and hot words. These are words that make people feel certain ways or stirs up specific emotions.

Power Words

Power words and phrases pack an unspoken punch when we use them in our stories, and they're a whole lot simpler than you think. Although there are hundreds of power words out there, we're only going to outline the main five over here. You already use all of these power words in everyday conversations, but through learning about their underlying effect, you'll be able to use them at key points in your stories to further your hypnotic effect. They are:

1. And

Links two thoughts together, bridging one idea to the next and ensuring that your listener will continue listening as you move through your story or from one story to the next.

2. Because

Says that what's coming up next is a reason. This has the effect of making your listener feel relaxed, because you are about to answer 'why' for them, even if they weren't asking why themselves. Like 'and', it also combines two things together which ensures that your audience will continue listening.

3. Which Means

Once again, the phrase "which means" helps the audience to relax. Through using this phrase, you make it clear that you know the answer and are going to give it to them, which means that they can stop stressing about knowing the answer themselves and relax into the next part of the story.

4. Imagine

When we ask our audience to imagine, it automatically activates their imaginations. This is key to transporting them away from reality and into our story for the time that we are talking, which in turn is vital to successfully hypnotizing them through our conversation.

5. Remember

Similar to when we ask someone to imagine, when we ask them to remember it kickstarts their subconscious mind and helps them to disconnect from reality. Our experiences might have taken place in the real world, but our memories exist separate from the conscious world.

Hot Words

While power words help our reader to disconnect from reality and relax into our story, hot words are those that carry an emotional charge. Hot words make our audience feel certain emotional responses, grabs their attention, and evokes a strong reaction from them. Once you have caused a response, you have committed your audience to partaking in the performance that is your conversation. Hot words are those that cause these emotive responses and "turn up the heat" of the conversation. We see examples of hot words in the sensationalist newspaper headlines that we are all bombarded with every day, because they're trying to shock us or anger us into buying the newspaper or clicking on the link to find out more.

Hot words are loaded with meaning, and their purpose is to get a reaction out of people. They include words like 'shocked', 'horrified', 'divine', and 'bliss'. Some examples of hot phrases are things like "I'd kill for another go", or "Let me set you free". To learn more hot words, just think of those words and phrases that carry a lot of emotion in their meaning, or read newspaper headlines and think about the way that the words they use make you feel. One final tip is that you should try not to overuse hot words in your conversations, because doing so will reduce their effect and make them seem more common. To maximize their impact, use hot words at specific points in your storytelling to ensure their full effect in your conversational hypnosis.

Recognize the Signs of the Hypnotized

Now that we've learned how to use the powerful technique of conversational hypnosis, it's time to learn about how to make sure that it's working for you. There are certain tell-tale signals that can help you to determine if the people you are speaking to are entranced by your story or if you need to change it up. Once you know what to look out for, it becomes pretty simple to spot if someone is both consciously and subconsciously listening to what you're saying. These signals are:

A Relaxed Body

The first sign that your audience is becoming hypnotized by your conversation is that their body is relaxed. If they are fidgeting, looking around, or constantly checking their phones, then you need to change up your approach.

Slow and Steady Breathing

The slower and steadier someone's breathing is, the more comfortable they are in your presence, and the more relaxed they're feeling. This means that they are primed to be hypnotized by your words, if they aren't already.

Dilated Pupils

Dilated pupils are a clear indicator that a person likes you. And, the more they like you, the more susceptible they are to being hypnotized by what you say and the way that you say it. If their eyes are softened, unfocused, or even wanting to close, these are also signs that they are entranced.

There you have it, my confident friend freshly made. A short but powerful chapter, and the final of our confidence keys, complete. Remember that you'll need to spend time understanding, practicing, and refining the tools, tips, tricks, and techniques I've taught you in this book to ensure your ultimate success. Embrace every interaction you have as a performance where you are the star of the show, embody your persona and make life your stage. This is the way to develop the mindset of power, influence, and success and will ultimately lead you to mastery in many more areas of your life.

CONCLUSION

Congratulations! You've made it to the end of our exploration on how to become the confident, powerful, and influential man of every woman's wildest dreams. Through putting in place the tried-and-tested techniques I've taught you in the seven keys that make up the different chapters of this book, and practicing them on a daily basis, you'll transform your personal relationships and professional life. More than that, though, you'll improve your mindset, upgrade your personality, and develop irresistible self-esteem. I did it, and so can you. Let's end off with a quick review of the different keys to success you've learned in this book.

KEYS TO SUCCESSFUL SELF-CONFIDENCE

1. Become fluent in the unspoken language of the body
2. Learn about how the human brain works and what women really want
3. Develop a persona that captures the new and improved you, and captivates everyone you come into contact with
4. Embrace the magic of the mind to conquer your limiting beliefs, reframe your perspective, and make your own luck
5. Internalize your personal power through developing your inner strength and honing your internal dialogue for successful self-confidence
6. Play the game of life in a cool, calm, and composed way that makes the most of the law of attraction
7. View every interaction like a performance where you are the stage master looking to captivate your audience and keep them engaged and entertained

Put these seven keys to successful self-confidence into practice today and see the positive results start to come your way. Know your confident personality and how to use it to your advantage, read the language of the body, and entrance the ladies with your wit and stories. This is the way to gain power, increase your influence, and successfully turn the life of your dreams into your reality.

REFERENCES

Blake, T. (2020). *How and Why Women Test Men.* Medium. https://medium.com/live-your-life-on-purpose/how-and-why-women-test-men-9ee93d5a6d53#:

Brazier, Y. (2016). *Mindfulness meditation helps to control emotions, says study.* Www.medicalnewstoday.com. https://www.medicalnewstoday.com/articles/313216#The-search-for-neural-associations-that-underlie-mindfulness

Buss, D. (2016). *The evolution of desire : strategies of human mating.* Basic Books.

Changing Minds. (2022). *Reframing.* Changingminds.org. http://changingminds.org/techniques/general/reframing.htm#:

Cherry, K. (2019). *How to Read Body Language and Facial Expressions.* Verywell Mind. https://www.verywellmind.com/understand-body-language-and-facial-expressions-4147228#:

D'Souza, R. (2015). *7 Facts You Need To Know About The Female Psyche.* IndiaTimes. https://www.indiatimes.com/lifestyle/self/7-facts-you-need-to-know-about-the-female-psyche-233934.html#:

Dena. (2016, June 23). *Own Your Success - Trust in Yourself and Attain Your Goals!* An Empowered Life. https://anempoweredlife.net/own-your-success/#:

Deschanel, D. (2020). *8 Tips to Smile with Confidence.* Health Constitution. https://www.healthconstitution.com.au/8-tips-to-smile-with-confidence/

Dumbleton, T. (2016). *How to Use the Law of Attraction.* Law of Attraction. https://lawofattractioni.com/use-law-attraction-2/

Fradet, N. (2012). *13 Revealing Body Language Hand Gestures.* Nicolas Fradet. https://nicolasfradet.com/hand-body-language/#:

Goswami, J. (2018). *Communicating with the Subconscious Mind - and Doing some Magic.* LinkedIn. https://www.linkedin.com/pulse/

communicating-subconscious-mind-doing-some-magic-jaydeep-h-goswami/

Interaction Design Foundation. (2021a). *Our Three Brains - The Emotional Brain*. The Interaction Design Foundation. https://www.interaction-design.org/literature/article/our-three-brains-the-emotional-brain#:

Interaction Design Foundation. (2021b). *The Concept of the "Triune Brain."* The Interaction Design Foundation. https://www.interaction-design.org/literature/article/the-concept-of-the-triune-brain#:

Komninos, A. (2017). *Our Three Brains - The Reptilian Brain*. The Interaction Design Foundation; UX courses. https://www.interaction-design.org/literature/article/our-three-brains-the-reptilian-brain

Komninos, A. (2020). *Our Three Brains - The Rational Brain*. The Interaction Design Foundation. https://www.interaction-design.org/literature/article/our-three-brains-the-rational-brain

Kosmotime. (2021a). *How To Get The Most Of Your Days: The Time Blocking Strategy*. KosmoTime. https://www.kosmotime.com/how-to-get-the-most-of-your-days-the-time-blocking-strategy/

Kosmotime. (2021b, August 12). *On Achieving Goals: Why Fulfillment Is More Important Than Drive*. KosmoTime. https://www.kosmotime.com/on-achieving-goals-why-fulfillment-is-more-important-than-drive/#:

Male Matter. (2020). *How to Achieve Your Goals and Potential Through Visualization*. Male Matter. https://malematter.com/visualization/

Matthews, D. (2020). *How to Identify Your Limiting Beliefs and Get Over Them*. Lifehack. https://www.lifehack.org/858652/limiting-beliefs#:

Miller, M. (2021). *Goals, Purpose and Meaning: What's the Difference?* Six Seconds. https://www.6seconds.org/2021/03/29/goals-purpose-and-meaning/

Neill, C. (2018). *Understanding Personality: The 12 Jungian Archetypes - Moving People to Action*. Conorneill.com. https://conorneill.com/

2018/04/21/understanding-personality-the-12-jungian-archetypes/#:

Pangilinan, E. (2020). *Life is an RPG*. Medium. https://medium.com/@emilpangilinan/life-is-an-rpg-ffb880a25790

Purple Pill Debate. (2022). *Women are biologically more selective than men*. Reddit. https://www.reddit.com/r/PurplePillDebate/comments/t29dmd/women_are_biologically_more_selective_than_men/

Robbins, T. (2022). *9 ways to cultivate inner strength and resilience*. Tonyrobbins.com. https://www.tonyrobbins.com/business/inner-strength/#:

Selig, M. (2016). *The 9 Superpowers of Your Smile*. Psychology Today. https://www.psychologytoday.com/us/blog/changepower/201605/the-9-superpowers-your-smile

Staniforth, J. (2022). *Create Your Own Luck by Using Affirmations*. Www.achieve-Goal-Setting-Success.com. https://www.achieve-goal-setting-success.com/create-your-own-luck.html#:

Thomas, J. (2022). *Unconfident Vs. Confident Body Language*. Www.betterhelp.com. https://www.betterhelp.com/advice/body-language/unconfident-vs-confident-body-language/

Weber, J. P. (2022). *The Power of Your Internal Dialogue*. Psychology Today. https://www.psychologytoday.com/us/blog/having-sex-wanting-intimacy/201707/the-power-your-internal-dialogue